FROM THE GALLEY

Stories and Recipes from American Mariners

MATTHEW BONVENTO

Copyright © 2025 by Good Wind Maritime Services

All rights reserved.

Published by Red Penguin Books

Bellerose Village, New York

ISBN

Print 978-1-63777-730-5

Digital 978-1-63777-729-9

No part of this book may be reproduced in any form or by any electronic or mechanical means, including information storage and retrieval systems, without written permission from the author, except for the use of brief quotations in a book review.

This book is dedicated to my amazing and supporting wife Danielle as well as my beautiful children Matteo and Arianna. Special thanks to my amazing family, Mom, Dad, Vicky, Chris, Marcus, Caroline, and Matthew.

CONTENTS

Introduction	xi
Galley Safety and Sanitation	xiii
Kitchen Conversions	xv

PART ONE
BREAKFAST

A Not So Everyday Omlette	3
French Toast Casserole	5
Homemade Scrapple	7
Grand Marnier French Toast	9
Shakshuka	10

PART TWO
APPETIZERS

Jalapeño Poppers	15
Lumpia	17
Hot Crab Dip	18
Crab Meat on English Muffin	19
Hot Crab Meat Cocktail Dip	20
Hot Spinach Dip	21
Portobelllo Mushroom Pizza	22
Smoked Salsa	24
French Onion Dip	26
Guacamole	28
Potato Pancakes	29
Roasted Shrimp with Feta	30
Reggie's Wedgies	32
Mystery Meat	34

PART THREE
SIDES

Pigtails and the Shipyard	37
Creamed Corn	43
Colette's Homemade Applesauce	44
Mac And Cheese	46
Corn Fritters	48

Orange Cauliflower: A vegetarian version of the popular Chinese orange chicken	50
Fermented Garlic Honey	52
Golden Family Chopped String Beans	53
Pan Fried Asparagus	55
Squash and Zuc	56
Twice Baked Potatoes	57
Braised Fried Cabbage	59
Rice With Raisins ~ Panamanian style	60
Corn & Cheese Casserole	62
Pop Elgin's Mashed Potatoes	63
Canlis Salad	66
Sautéed Sauerkraut	68

PART FOUR
SAUCES AND MARINADES

Cranberry Sauce	71
Shish-ka-Bab Marinade	72
Ugly Sauce	73
Dry Ribs Rub	74
Dry Ribs Rub	75
Putanesca Sauce	76
Surviving the Night Shift	77

PART FIVE
SOUP AND STEW

Lentil Stew	83
Cream of Peanut Soup	85
Cheddar Broccoli Soup	86
Clam Chowder	88
Hamburger Barley Vegetable Soup	90
Instant Pot Chicken Soup	91
Egg Drop Soup	93
Bean and Pasta Soup	94
Chioppino Italian Fisherman's Soup	96
Norwegian Lapskaus	98
Chicken Souse – A Bahamian Classic	99
Skipperhuset's Fish Chowder	101
Chicken Soup	104
Matzah Ball and Chicken Soup	106
Fat Kid Party	108

PART SIX
DINNER

WhaHappen to Old Bay	113
Homestyle Puerto Rican Red Beans	115
Homestyle Puerto Rican Pollo Guisado	118
Mella's Meatballs	121
Zwiebelkuchen	123
Chili	126
Country Fried Steak	128
Slow Cooker Mushroom Chicken	130
Chicken Satay with Peanut Sauce	132
Chicken Marsala	134
Pulled Pork Sliders	136
Kielbasa Casserole	138
Smokey Cajon Hamburger	139
Taco/Pasta Casserole	141
Quick Goulash	142
Dad's Black Forest Chicken with BBC Sauce	143
Enchilada Casserole	145
Vegan Sloppy Joe's	146
Farro Risotto with Shrimp	148
Heart Healthy Shrimp Scampi	150
Pan Seared Scallops	152
Tin Foil Fish Grill	154
Smoked Fish And Smoked Fish Salad	156
Capt Paul's Fishcakes	158
Crab Boil	160
Beer Boiled Fish	162
Ginger Scallion Shrimp	163
Grilled Tilefish	165
Spicy Seared Sea Scallops	167
Honey Garlic Shrimp	168
Yum Neau or Larb Neau or Larb Gai Yum Neau or Larb Neau or Larb Gai	170
Meatloaf	173
Chicken Golden Curry Recipe	174
Coconut Curry In a Hurry Recipe	176
Goulash	178
Gumbo	180
Brisket	182
Grilled Cheese Sandwich with Pickles	183

PART SEVEN
DESSERT

Chocolate Roll	189
Grilled Peaches	191
Quick Dessert	192
Tugboat Rice Pudding	193
Apple and Pear Cake with Pine Nuts	195
French Chocolate Cake	197
Jacobine Kake from 1919	199
Tilslørte Bondepiker	201
Snickerdoodle	203
Zucchini Bread	205
Greek Milk Pie	207
Purple Plum Torte	209
Impossible Pie	211
Maritime M.U.G. Cupcake	212
The Centeno Family's "New Yorican Cheesecake Flan"	214
Chocolate Cake	216
Peanut Butter-Chocolate No-Bake Cookies	218
Chocolate Peppermint Brownies	220
Banana Pudding Recipe	222
Hot Curried Fruit	224
Sour Cream Pecan Pie	225
Grape Pie	226
Rum Cake	227
Butterscotch Brownies	229

PART EIGHT
SNACKS

Shortbread cookies	233
South of the Border Mix	235
Asian flavored snack mix	237
Snack Mix Extraordinaire	239
Maxine	241

PART NINE
DRINKS

Sun Tea	247
Viking Eggnog	248
Hooch	250
Green Monster	251

Kahlua	252
Mulled Cider	253
Mulled Wine	254
Preparing for Sea	255
Life on Board	259
The Team	261
Communication on Board	265
Acknowledgements	269
Let There Be No Moaning at the Bar	273

INTRODUCTION
THOMAS POWERS

I started a new career in the Maritime industry working for McAllister Towing of NY harbor. I had just received my able seaman ticket. I didn't know what I was going to expect when walking on a vessel that I had never been on and didn't know what to do. So I'm walking around getting to know the crew, learning my watch schedule and getting to know the lay of the boat and their operations. Now knowing what to do and how to do it, the captain asked me a very important question. "Hey, kid, do you know how to cook?" I didn't know how to answer. My reaction was like a deer looking in a headlight, because I never cooked besides BBQ. So the captain got his answer by my facial reaction. So he goes, "Well, kid, it's sink or swim because on your watch schedule you're in charge of cooking." I was so shocked. I didn't know what in the hell I was going to do and just thinking when I was at home, the only person that cooked was my mother. Eight months before my day of hire, my mother passed away. So I couldn't even fall back on what to do for recipes or any advice. So I go down into the galley to see what the crew had on the board. After hours looking, I'm saying to myself I'm screwed, spinning my phone off the table on saying how am I going to get through these two weeks without getting kicked off, and all of a sudden, it hit me. The answers were to my phone, so I started looking up things on how to cook but finally found an app called "tasty." I tell you what, that app has saved my rear end. The food didn't come out 100% perfect, but the crew always had full belly, and that's what matter to me the most.

GALLEY SAFETY AND SANITATION

It is very important to ensure that all cookware is kept clean. When in doubt, re-clean cookware in hot water with antibacterial soap.

- Before handling food and utensils, after handling any raw meats and eggs, if you sneeze or cough, cut your hands, or use the head, wash your hands thoroughly before touching anything food related.

- Keep all utensils and cookware clean. When washing, dry with paper towels.

- Regularly clean the galley and all appliances.

- Regularly change out sponges and dishrags.

- Keep all knives sharp. Dull blades cause more injuries than do sharp ones.

KITCHEN CONVERSIONS

U.S. Units	Canadian Metric	Australian Metric
¼ tsp	1 ml	1 ml
½ tsp	2 ml	2 ml
1 tsp	5 ml	5 ml
1 tbls	15 ml	20 ml
¼ cup	50 ml	60 ml
⅓ cup	75 ml	80 ml
½ cup	125 ml	125 ml
⅔ cup	150 ml	170 ml
¾ cup	175 ml	190 ml
1 cup	250 ml	250 ml
1 quart	1 liter	1 liter
1 ½ quarts	1.5 liters	1.5 liters
2 quarts	2 liters	2 liters
2 ½ quarts	2.5 liters	2.5 liters
3 quarts	3 liters	3 liters
4 quarts	4 liters	4 liters
1 ounce	30 grams	30 grams
2 ounces	55 grams	60 grams
3 ounces	85 grams	90 grams
4 ounces (¼ pound)	115 grams	125 grams
8 ounces (½ pound)	225 grams	225 grams
16 ounces (1 pound)	455 grams	500 grams

Farenheit	Celsius
32	0
212	100
250	120
275	140
300	150
325	160
350	180
375	190
400	200
425	220
450	230
475	240
500	260

Inches	Centimeters
1	2.5
2	5.0
3	7.5
4	10.0
5	12.5
6	15.0
7	17.5
8	20.5
9	23.0
10	23.5
11	28.0
12	30.5
13	33.0

Equivalent Measures

3 tsp	1 tbsp
4 tbsp	¼ cup
5 tbsp + 1 tsp	⅓ cup
8 tbsp	½ cup
12 tbsp	¾ cup
16 tbsp	1 cup (8 ounces)
2 cups	1 pint (16 ounces)
4 cups	1 quart (2 pints/32 ounces)
8 cups	½ gallon (4 pints/64 ounces)
4 quarts	1 gallon (128 ounces)

Common abbreviations

Degrees	* or dg	package	pkg
Dozen	doz	pint	pt
Gallon	gal	pound	lb or #
Hour	hr	quart	qt
Minute	min	teaspoon	tsp or t
Ounce	oz	tablespoon	tbsp or T
inch	in.	second	sec

PART ONE
BREAKFAST

All of the names have been changed for the privacy of the people involved, but everything in this story actually happened.

I was stationed on the Sodermand, and we were making a stop in the Netherlands for cargo ops. While we were there, the crew was able to take a little shore leave. Now, anyone that has spent any amount of time in the Netherlands knows that there are various activities and plenty of ways to spend your time and money. In my case, my interests tended to lean towards architecture, culture, and local cuisine. Some of my other ship mates had "different" interests. The subject of this story (we'll call him Tiny) had a very specific mindset and a particular, shall we say, drive.

Well, one afternoon, a number of crew members caught the shuttle that brought us from the ship into town. On one of my previous outings, I had come across a quaint pub that had wicked good food. One of the other cool draws of this particular venue was their mascot... A giant bull mastiff (his name was Big Mike). Hands down, one of the coolest dogs I have ever had the pleasure of knowing. Well, the only way to get to and from this particular pub was to travel through the Red Light District. Like I said, there were a number of crew members who were heading with us to this pub, but not all of them made it "to the pub." (I trust a translation is not necessary).

Tiny was among the crew that was joining us but was led astray. Well, Tiny liked to barter. Point of fact, he thought of it as a great game. He introduced himself to a lovely young redhead named Lucile and began the 'discussion' as it were. We watched this gab session with interest and, quite frankly, amusement. After about five minutes of the conversation, I had seen enough. Especially when Tiny's latest bid was 50 Euro and a bag of Doritos . . . I was aghast and shook my head in disbelief. I led the rest of the crew who were accompanying me to the pub. We spent about three hours enjoying local cuisine, local brews, and playing with Big Mike. When it was time to go, we had to walk back through the red light district to get back to where the shuttle was picking us up. While passing through the district, I started laughing hysterically. Our Bosun, Terry, asked me what was so funny. All I could do was point and say 1 word . . .Doritos!!! There was Lucile, sitting in her window, enjoying a giant bag of Doritos!!!

Keith Gibney

A NOT SO EVERYDAY OMLETTE

Ingredients:

3 large eggs
½ tsp. finely minced onion (fresh or dried)
½ finely minced fresh garlic
Dash of paprika
Small pinch of parsley
Dash of Adobo
Small pinch sea salt
½ tsp. fresh ground black pepper
2 dashes of hot pepper sauce (optional, for an extra kick)
¼ lb. fresh mushrooms
¼ cup chopped ham slices
¼ cup shredded cheese (advise Swiss or Muenster. Pepperjack for a kick)

Directions:

1. Heat a wide sauté pan on low flame with 1 tbsp. olive oil. When warm (not hot) throw the onions and garlic in and constantly move around until lightly brown.

2. Throw in the mushrooms and again constantly keep everything moving and well mixed. You should just begin to get the smell of mushroom and lightly browned.
3. Take out of pan, into a small bowl, and put aside.
4. Crack the eggs into a mixing bowl and add ingredients #4 – 9, above.
5. Whisk very briskly but for *no more* than a minute.
6. Heat the same pan used for the mushroom and add two tsp of olive oil or butter over a medium flame.
7. Monitor the pan very carefully–when very warm (not hot) add eggs and let settle into the pan. When it looks as if the bottom is forming up but there is still liquid egg, slide one side over and tilt the pan so the liquid egg runs into the open space. Repeat until all liquid egg is gone.
8. Turn over omelette quickly and add the ham, cheese, and mushrooms. Fold over and serve on a preheated plate.

FRENCH TOAST CASSEROLE

Ingredients:

1 lb. loaf cinnamon raison bread, cubed
4 oz. cream cheese, cubed
8 eggs, beaten
1½ cup half and half
¼ cup sugar
½ cup maple syrup
2 tbsp. vanilla
1 tbsp. cinnamon

Directions:

1. Place half of the bread cubes in a greased 9x13 pan, top with cubed cream cheese and remaining bread.
2. Mix remaining ingredients in a bowl, pour over the top of bread, cover with aluminum foil, and refrigerate for 6-8 hours.
3. Pre-heat oven to 350 degrees.
4. Remove casserole from fridge for 30 minutes and then bake in pre-heated oven for 30 minutes.

5. Remove aluminum foil cover and bake another 15-20 minutes until knife can come out of the center clean.

HOMEMADE SCRAPPLE

Ingredients:

1 19 oz. package plain bratwurst links (casings removed)
1 16 oz. roll breakfast sausage
2½ cups water
¼ tsp. smoked sea salt
¼ tsp. onion powder
¼ tsp. garlic powder
¼ tsp. ground thyme
¼ tsp. ground marjoram
¼ tsp. ground coriander seed
¼ tsp. ground cayenne pepper
1 tsp. ground sage
1 cup yellow corn meal
1½ cup white corn meal
1 tsp. coarse black pepper

Directions:

1. Remove bratwurst casings and place into a 10" camp oven. Add roll of sausage. Add water.

2. Over high heat, bring to a boil, while mashing meat with a fork, for about 10 minutes. Add all seasonings except black pepper, continually stirring for about 5 minutes.
3. Remove from heat and let cool for 10 minutes. Pour mixture into a blender and pulse until finely ground. Pour mixture back into oven, reduce to low heat, and stir in black pepper.
4. Whisk in corn meal, stirring until mixture is very thick. (Whisk should stand up.)
5. Pour mixture into a loaf pan. Cover and chill overnight. (Freeze if not used within a week.)
6. Heat cast iron skillet over medium high, add oil, and fry for approximately 5 minutes per side or until nicely browned on each side.

GRAND MARNIER FRENCH TOAST

Ingredients:

6 eggs
2 tbsp. sugar
½ cups heavy cream
1 tsp. vanilla
1 shot Grand Marnier
12 slices of stale french bread about ½" thick

Directions:

1. Blend eggs and sugar together. Add cream and beat at low speed for 2 minutes. Add vanilla and Grand Marnier.
2. Lay bread on tray and pour sauce over. Flip bread to the other side.
3. Let stand overnight. Fry in butter.

SHAKSHUKA

Ingredients:

1 white onion, diced
1 jalapeño pepper
3 tbsp. minced garlic
2 tsp. sweet paprika
1 tsp. cumin
¾ tbsp. black pepper
½ tsp. salt
1½ cans of 15 ounce whole peeled tomatoes
8 large eggs
1 tsp. cayenne pepper

Directions:

1. Sauté onions, garlic, and jalapeño pepper (the earlier/later that you add the peppers will vary the spiciness).
2. Add crushed tomatoes. Season with salt, pepper, sweet paprika, a little sugar (especially if tomatoes are acidic), cumin (if desired).

3. Cook a few minutes to marry flavors.
4. Make a well in the pan to add eggs.
5. Cook and cover until eggs are done to desired consistency.
6. Goes well with crusty bread and an Israeli Salad.

PART TWO
APPETIZERS

CAPTAIN PATRICK MICHAEL DECHARLES II

Right out of Texas Maritime Academy, the jobs were few and far between. A few of us sailed foreign flag to get some sea time, which counts if you do it correctly. I sailed for Del Monte on the east coast, making runs to Central and South America carrying bananas. This was not a containership but an actual refrigeration ship that hauled 495,000 of 20 kilo boxes. On every watch, we had to go down in the holds and take pulp temperatures to ensure they were OK and the ventilation was correct (53.5 degrees F for Cavendish bananas). The vessel had 18 different nationalities on board. Spanish and English were the common languages.

We had a Cuban American Radio Operator aboard (Sparks). I, being the lowly 3rd Mate, had the 8-12 watch. Every morning at 0900, Sparks would come to the bridge with his Cuban coffee and give me the weather report. The weather report in those days was the old style weather report where you had to plot the lows and highs and the frontal systems (no facsimile). He would always tell anyone who would listen how he hated Castro over and over again.

We were headed south from Galveston or Tampa to Puerto Barrio in Guatemala (a shit hole). Anyway, we were passing between Yucatan, Mexico, and Cape San Antonio, Cuba. I had on a previous trip when calling in Tampa went into an army/navy store and bought fatigues that resemble the outfit that Castro was always picture in. At the time I had a full beard and mustache. As we approached Cape San Antonio to take a bearing and just before Sparks would make his daily call on the bridge, I changed into my Castro gear with cigar to top it off. Needless to say, when he came to the bridge, he went nuts, screaming to the ole man. The ole man took it in stride as he was Irish, but told me not upset Sparks too much in the future. The rest of the crew loved it.

JALAPEÑO POPPERS

Ingredients:

10 jalapeños
8 oz. cream Cheese
8 oz. brick of yellow sharp cheddar
¾ lb. of bacon
24 12 oz. cans of beer for personal consumption

Directions:

1. Get a bunch of fresh poppers, cut them in half & clean them.
2. Oil up a tray and place poppers in oven at 350 degrees for 20 minutes.
3. At same time, cook bacon in oven.
4. After 20 minutes is up, crush all the bacon.
5. In a bowl put cream cheese & shredded cheddar cheese.
6. Put bowl in microwave to soften up cream cheese & semi melt cheddar cheese.
7. Then take crumbled bacon & mix in bowl.
8. Then spoon the mixture from the bowl into each half of the canoe looking poppers.
9. When finished, place the poppers on tray, shred more cheddar cheese over all the poppers. Place in oven & broil until the cheddar cheese on top is crispy. Final step is to take out of oven to cool off, eat & wash it down with any cold beer.

LUMPIA

Ingredients:

1 lb. ground pork
½ onion
2 stalk celery
2 long carrots
1 tbsp. salt
1 tbsp. pepper
1 egg
Package of eggroll wrappers
Sweet and sour spring roll sauce

Directions:

Mix ingredients together (except wrappers). Wrap in the wrappers and deep fry.

HOT CRAB DIP
PAT BLOSS

Ingredients:

2 lb. crabmeat
1 small onion
3 tbsp. butter
2 tbsp. horseradish
1 tbsp. Old Bay
1 (8 oz.) cream cheese
1 cup sour cream
Ritz cracker crumbs (optional)

Directions:

1. Finely chip onion. Sauté onion in butter. Add horseradish, Old Bay, crab, cream cheese and sour cream. Simmer (low heat) and stir until smooth.
2. Pour into baking dish and top with cracker crumbs.
3. Bake at 350 degrees until golden brown on top (about 10-15 minutes).

CRAB MEAT ON ENGLISH MUFFIN

Ingredients:

6 English muffins, halved
16 oz. crab meat, drained
1 stick butter
15 oz. jar draft cheddar
2 tbsp. mayonnaise
½ tsp. garlic salt
Bit of Sherry

Directions:

Blend all ingredients together and spread on muffin halves. Quarter and then freeze. Bake at 425 degrees for about 12 minutes.

HOT CRAB MEAT COCKTAIL DIP

Ingredients:

7 oz. crab meat
3 3 oz. cream cheese packages with chives
2 tbsp. mayonnaise
3 tbsp. chopped onions

Directions:

Blend all ingredients together. Bake at 350 degrees for 25-30 minutes or until bubbly.

HOT SPINACH DIP

Ingredients:

1 pkg. frozen chopped spinach, thawed
1 8oz. package cream cheese, thawed
½ cup mayonnaise
⅓ cup grated parmesan cheese
6-8 slices bacon, cooked and crumbled
2-3 green onions, chopped
1 tbsp. chopped fresh parsley
2 tsp. lemon juice

Directions:

1. Drain spinach.
2. Combine spinach and remaining ingredients in a large bowl; stir well.
3. Spoon into a greased shallow 1 qt baking dish.
4. Bake uncovered at 350 degrees for 20-25 minutes or until thoroughly heated.
5. Serve with crackers.

PORTOBELLLO MUSHROOM PIZZA

Ingredients:

6 portobello caps, stemmed
2 tbsp. olive oil
1 medium onion, chopped
1 clove garlic, minced
12 oz. Italian sausage meat, no casing
3 medium tomatoes (peeled, diced, and seeded)
1 tsp. chopped fresh oregano (1/2 dried)
¾ cup shredded mozzarella

Directions:

1. Clean mushrooms by scraping gills off of the inside.
2. Preheat oven to 375 degrees.
3. Sprinkle salt and pepper on mushroom, put on baking sheet inside down.
4. Bake until liquid comes out of the mushroom, about 10 to 15 minutes.
5. Warm oil in a large skillet. Add onion, cook until softened.

Add garlic, cook for 1 minute. Add sausage cook until no longer pink.
6. Stir in tomatoes and cook until liquid evaporates. Place mixture in each cap, topping with cheese.
7. Bake until cheese is melted. About 10 minutes.

SMOKED SALSA

Ingredients:

4 Roma tomatoes, blanched
½ sweet onion
¼ green bell pepper
5 garlic cloves
2 jalapeño peppers
1 habanero pepper
3 peach slices (canned in syrup) – save syrup for later
1 lime, squeezed
1 tbsp. cilantro

1 tsp. each black pepper, salt, and cumin
1 tbsp. honey
3 tbsp. reserved peach syrup

Directions:

1. Heat smoker to 200 degrees with Apple or Pecan Chips.
2. Cut out part of tomato where the stem attaches, drop in boiling water for about a minute or smoke at 225 for about 20 minutes (or until skin easily comes off). Move directly to ice water to cool off and stop the cooking.
3. Smoke tomatoes, onion, garlic, peppers and peaches for 1 ½ hours.
4. Add all ingredients to food processor and pulse until desired texture.

FRENCH ONION DIP

Ingredients:

2 tbsp. olive oil
1 medium onion, finely chopped
2 garlic cloves, finely grated
2 sprigs, thyme
3 shallots, finely chopped
1 white onion
1 red onion
1 cup sour cream
¼ cup chives, finely chopped
1 tbsp. lemon juice
Kosher salt
Freshly ground pepper
Kettle cooked potato chips and fresh cut vegetables, for serving

Directions:

1. Heat oil in a small skillet over medium. Cook onion, garlic, and thyme stirring occasionally until onion is deep golden brown and very soft, about 35-40 minutes. Discard thyme and let cool.

2. Mix caramelized onions, chives, sour cream, shallots, and lemon juice in a medium bowl.
3. Season with salt and pepper.
4. Let sit for 30 minutes to allow flavors to meld before serving.

GUACAMOLE

Ingredients:

6 avocados
1 clove garlic
1 lime
1 tomato chopped up fine
Coriander
Salt

Directions:

1. Chop garlic or put it through a press, mix with tomatoes. Add salt to tomatoes. Chop fresh coriander if you have it, do not bother with dried.
2. Halve avocados, remove pits, and make a few slices in avocados. Add half lime to avocado center and then scoop out into bowl. If not serving right away, add pits to mixture and cover with plastic wrap over the surface or it will brown. If you like spice, add slivers of jalapeños and slivers of red onion, but not too much.

POTATO PANCAKES

Ingredients:

2 lbs. Idaho potatoes
½ cup flour
1 egg
Salt to taste
¼ lb. of butter

Directions:

1. Grate potatoes and mix all ingredients together. Beat well.
2. Bake on greaseless hot griddle. Place 1½ tbsp. of batter, spread thin. Cook on both sides.
3. When all batter is used up, brown ¼ lb. of butter and spread on both sides of the pancakes.

ROASTED SHRIMP WITH FETA

Ingredients:

1½ cups of diced fennel (1 bulb)
1 tbsp. minced garlic (3 cloves)
¼ cup dry white wine
1 (14.5 ounce) can diced tomatoes, drained
2 tsp. tomato paste
1 tsp. dried oregano
1 tbsp. PernodKosher salt and freshly ground black pepper

1¼ lbs. (16 to 18) shrimp, peeled and deveined (with tails left on); I use Costco cooked frozen)
3 oz. feta cheese (coarsely crumbled
1 cup fresh bread crumbs (I use Progresso Italian bread crumbs)
1 tbsp. minced fresh parsley
1 tsp. grated lemon zest
2 lemons

Directions:

1. Pre-heat oven 400 degrees.
2. Heat 2 tbsp. of good olive oil in 10 or 12 inch heavy ovenproof skillet over med-low heat. Add the fennel and garlic and sauté for 8 to 10 minutes until tender. Add the wine and bring to a boil, scraping up any browned bits clinging to the bottom of skillet, and cook until the liquid is reduced by half, 2 to 3 minutes.
3. Add the tomatoes, tomato paste, oregano, Pernod, 1 tsp. salt, and ½ tsp. pepper to skillet. Simmer over low heat, stirring occasionally for 10 to 15 minutes.
4. Slightly brown the bread crumbs in oil, add the parsley and lemon zest. Arrange the shrimp artfully in one layer over the tomato mixture in the **skillet** and top with bread crumb mixture, sprinkle feta on top. Bake in same **skillet** dish for about 15 minutes if using raw shrimp.
5. **Or** if using cooked shrimp can be heated for 2 minutes in the microwave before topping with the browned bread crumbs and feta. (It can be made the day before if using cooked shrimp. Just wait to add the bread crumbs and feta before serving.) Bon Appetite!

Taste tested by alumni with rave reviews. (Adapted from the Barefoot Contessa!)

REGGIE'S WEDGIES

Ingredients:

1 cup ripe chopped ripe olives (you can now buy the small cans already chopped)
½ cup THINLY sliced green onions
1½ cup shredded SHARP cheddar cheese
½ cup mayonnaise
½ tsp. salt
½ tsp. curry powder

Directions:

1. Spread mixture on toasted English muffin halves.
2. Bake at 325 degrees for 15 minutes, remove and cut wedges in quarters!
3. They can also be broiled till the cheese melts.

MYSTERY MEAT

Ingredients:

½ lb. swiss cheese - grated
1 small green pepper - chopped
1 small onion - chopped
½ cup green olives - chopped

Directions:

1. Mix all with mayonnaise till it sticks together!!
2. Serve with crackers.

PART THREE
SIDES

PIGTAILS AND THE SHIPYARD

This sea story is about a green 3rd assistant engineer and her first shipyard period. The setting was wintertime 2003 in Spain. Most real names have been omitted.

Memories can be tricky; the good ones do stick with a person for a lifetime. PTSD has a way of protecting a person's brain and blocking out the bad memories. So, for this story we will stick to a few good memories. Such as the first time I remember eating spaghetti, covered head to toe because I couldn't shovel it in my mouth fast enough while sitting in my highchair at my mother's house. Or the sports memories from my youth stick with me so vividly. Sometimes regardless of my age these memories fill my head while I sleep, and I could be scoring a goal or kicking a penalty shot. For instance, one time I kicked a ball in my sleep and sharply kicked my boyfriend dead smack in his face. I do not blame him for that breakup, to say the least. I keep most stories to myself, except the occasional bar tail.

This one, however, brings truth to one of the many reasons I sailed for so long and leads to why I have been single most of my adult life. Finding passion and people that treated me as if I mattered and the magnitude of the little things that sweep through my face to make me smile is sometimes flattering and magical but fleeting. I am willing to wait because my worth is more powerful than settling for mediocrity. To understand my story, I shall set the mood.

Standing in the control room of my first ship, I was in a white tee shirt and denim overalls, my hair neatly parted in pigtails, I was in all my glory. I was a youthful 23 as the day was long, having enough energy to power a city. Young and dumb in a way, but the wisdom of an old man. My pockets filled with every sensible engineer's 'rates', a flashlight, accompanied by a pen, notebook, and adjustable wrench. I had never gone to a dry-dock before and wasn't aware of the magnitude of what occurs during a haul-out. I simply showed up to watch and did as I was told.

There is a chain of command on merchant vessels and although as a 3rd engineer, I was a graduate of the esteemed SUNY Maritime college, dues still had to be paid, sweat poured, and goals reached in order to learn and gain the respect of fellow shipmates. I had never even seen a slow speed diesel up close or worked on a diesel engine. Possibly a lab with Combat Klein carefully over my shoulder or Chief Baumgart showing videos yelling at me for any given reason. Charlie Munch would bring in small scale models that would impress us as they would work, but nothing on the magnitude of being able to walk into an engine. I was 100% steam in my blood and veins all four years at Maritime.

I was greener then green, but eager to learn. Often scared to ask questions. My chief engineer was a graduate of Kings Point, a former rugby player who wore military camo pants and a black tee shirt every day. He was big in stature and not easy to get along with. If I asked a question, he would yell; if I sat at the wrong table, he would give me a dirty look. It took two years to gain his respect. The first engineer looked more like Santa clause, very inappropriate and made me feel as if he was always picturing me naked. In fact, one day while in the engine room I remember vividly that "Cheeseburger in Paradise" was playing on the CD player. He pretended to slip as the ship lightly swayed, his hand tracing my entire breast in a vertical creepy matter. But this is a happy story, so I digress. The only one that suffered was my love for Jimmy Buffet. I still cringe when I hear a song by him.

This memory is as if Lin-Manual himself wrote the musical to my memories. If there was ever a Disney Princess that was an engineer I fit the role, however, I always felt like the ugly duckling. Looking back at the pictures, I see a fit strong woman who had fought body issues and conquered more in 18 years than most people had their entire lives, I was stunning and yet I didn't even know it.

The ship had just arrived at the shipyard in Spain. Unaware of how many people were coming to help overhaul engines and generators, experts from all over the States and Spain, Romania, and London, the list of service suppliers was massive. I didn't know they were coming. Every time we pulled into port, the crew onboard had to do all the maintenance and repairs. I was a blank slate at this point and wildly energetic as this was a first experience. I was a bit tired from the journey from Baltimore, Maryland to Europe, but I recovered quickly.

To continue my story, I was on a late watch in the engine room, it was empty, I was standing in my overalls, pigtails; looking at the controls and filling out the logbook when a man walked in swiftly. Freshly out of the shower, I could smell his scent as he walked by me not even knowing I was there at first. I turned around and his eyes met mine from across the room, he gave me that Cheshire cat smile that I could tell he was pleasantly surprised and a little taken back that this marvelous creature was standing before him. A soft "Oh, hello" came from his lips and I said, "Hello there can I help you?" After all, this was my territory. He told me his name and I politely smiled and said welcome. He was not very tall, but he was masculine and handsome. He assumed I was Spanish as most men do and spoke to me in Spanish. I say my famous saying, "No Comprende Nada Nunka," which loosely translates to I don't understand anything ever. It usually makes the person laugh as my 2 years of Spanish in high school did not stick. His voice was strong and had a deep vibrato that makes any female choir/acapella nerd very happy. It was not love at first sight, but a bond was formed in that instant. He explained that he was there to overhaul the generators and aid the vessel as he had worked on the sister ships. He befriended me instantly. He told me that he had a house in Spain and the US, explained his experience in the industry, and suggested he would love to show me the ropes if time allowed.

The shipyard period was roughly 15 to 20 days, each day was 12-hour days. I would weld, change out valves, pack new valves, solder, fix electrical cords, lights, fixtures, work on the shit tank. I cleaned, repaired and maintained equipment non-stop. I always smelled like simple green or diesel fuel with a hint of body wash and sweat. When I walked in an engine room at first, I never considered that each valve had to be reconditioned or replaced, and being the 3rd engineer, a lot of that work fell on me. The amount of gasket materials used in a shipyard was shocking to me.

I did have help, shipyard workers are a blessing and a curse, they filled the bilges day and night. I came to find out if left alone to their own devises they could quickly become obnoxious, I would have to bend down at the knees so they wouldn't make comments about my ass or boobs. The first rule at a shipyard is never leave your tools out or they will be stolen by the end of the shift, always lock your doors and keep anything of value hidden. The blessing part falls on every heavy piece of equipment they would help out when told, the workers were quick to take off nuts and bolts, all while having a remarkable sense of humor.

Not being able to communicate in those days a lot of pointing with flashlights happen. After about 10 days or so, they finally stopped, looking at me as only a sex object but showed me love and respect. These guys would sit in bilges covered in dirt and grease head to toe with their friends, dad's and cousins. They showed me some tricks that most engineers my age weren't doing. I paid attention, learned as the shipyard days and nights were long.

One of the last nights in the shipyard I walked to the lower engine room to check in on things before I finally got a chance to see the city. The Spanish guys on this shift were very excited to see me, sad to see me go once the shipyard was over, they stopped me for a moment. They flipped over their white dirty buckets and it was as if Nick Cannon and his entire drumline came alive under the bilges. In unison the beating was spectacular, all together they started singing in Spanish and beating their drums. Time stood still for those few minutes, and I just watched in awe.

Two of my favorite things in this world became music and engine rooms together. As the drum major for 4 years of my high school Marching Band, I could not have been happier in that moment. The engine room drums filled the entire space. Using their wrenches and hands as drum sticks the men sang three songs to me and thanked me for treating them so nice. I blushed so hard I had a headache from smiling.

Later that night my new friend asked me to go to dinner. I was not sure if it was a date or if he was trying to be a big brother type. At this point, he was very overprotective of me. After countless hours of shining a flashlight for each other, we ate meals together, we worked on the generators together in seamless synchronicity. A shipyard is almost like basic training, many hate it, many quit. The ones that do stick it out can learn from the experience or never want to go back.

It was winter and very cold, almost looked like snow that night. As I scrubbed the grease from my hands with an engineer's best friend diesel oil, butterflies filled my stomach. I did carefully pack a few outfits that didn't make me look like a tomboy. Still unsure if this was a date, at that point I didn't care really, I wanted to get off the ship. Having a Spanish/American tour guide for the night I was excited to say the least. I could see the sights and I had a personal translator and guide.

He was very well dressed, as was I, we went to a very nice mom and pop place for dinner. I never had meat that thinly sliced before. Meats filled the room as they were hung up vertically with care row by row. The smell of balsamic and fresh bread, garlic, handsome cuts of steak being seared on the stove top filled the room. The townspeople were loud and jovial, they moved slowly and with elegance. The entire dinner took over two hours as we enjoyed each course. There wasn't a need for fast service when the only entertainment needed was the person you are with. Cell phones weren't iPhone and Samsung, they were simple. I was just out of college by a year, so I was still in a beer phase, however, he ordered wine. He was elegant and older. He was passionate, sweet, and poured my wine. He held my door open, moved my chair so I could gingerly sit. When I went to the bathroom he stood up. Wait what! I had only seen that in the movies. There was a moment at the end of the night while we waited for the taxi, I closed my eyes while we were huddled together freezing. I could smell his cologne. It was expensive and sultry, that smell mixed with his black leather jacket made my 5 senses all at once go into overdrive. He slowly leaned in and kissed me softly on the lips and embraced me.

We closed the night by going to meet some of the English contractors at a local pub. These guys didn't even recognize me without my pigtails, and oversized clothing. A stronger more independent woman stood before them, no longer the green engineer that was tracing pipes. One of the elders looked at me and said, "I am proud of you kid." He raised his pint glass and started singing "Oh the Crystal Chandelier…" All his mates joined in as they surrounded me in a tiny shipyard pub, with more history plastered on the walls and traditions filled with sea stories for multiple lifetimes. My heart swelled for the second or possibly third time that day. I was filled with joy, passion, wonder, and surprise as the Charley Pride song was shouted out with English accents.

The day filled with Spanish shipyard workers beating on buckets, a very sweet dinner with a lifelong friend, which we have remained friends over the years, a night filled with boisterous blokes who turned my name into the sweetest of melodies. The rest of the story you'll have to wait and sea-as there are many more memories from this female chief engineer.

Mrs. Crystal Allen Craft

CREAMED CORN

Ingredients:

2 tbsp. butter
2 cups corn kernels
2 tbsp. minced shallot
¾ cup lowfat milk
2 tsp. flour
¼ tsp. salt

Directions:

1. Melt butter in saucepan.
2. Add corn and shallot, cooking for 1 minute, stir constantly
3. Add milk, salt, and flour.
4. Bring to a boil.
5. Reduce heat to low, cover, cook for four minutes.

COLETTE'S HOMEMADE APPLESAUCE

ANDREW HIGGINS

As a child growing up, during every holiday me and all of my cousins and family always looked forward especially to one thing, my grandma Colette's applesauce! Every holiday it was a highlight of ours, after coming back inside from playing a various amount of sports and games. We'd always come running inside for some of her delicious applesauce, and while eating it always joking around and just making incredible memories that I still cherish to this day. To say the least, this applesauce has been the centerpiece to countless memories and always left us smiling and FULL!

This simple crowd pleaser is an old recipe that has evolved over generations of my family. The measurements below are approximate; it really can't be messed up. All you have to do is adjust it to suit your tastes—less or more sugar, less or more cinnamon, thinner or chunkier, etc.

Ingredients:

5 lbs. of apples, any type or a mix
Cinnamon (about a tbsp.)
Sugar (about 1-2 tbsp.)
Raisins (about a cup)

Dried cranberries (about a cup)
Water (about 2 cups)

Directions:

1. Peel, core and slice the apples. Place in a large pot. Add about 12-16 ounces of water, a tablespoon of cinnamon and a scoop of sugar. (Go easy on the sugar as the dried fruit adds sweetness. You can add a little more sugar later on if you like). As these are approximate measures, add water, cinnamon and sugar gradually, and adjust to your taste. Simmer and stir to break up the apples. <u>Keep stirring until done.</u> The more water you add, the thinner the applesauce will be. The more cinnamon, the darker the color.
2. When the apples start to break up and dissolve, add about a cup of raisins and a cup of craisins. Again, adjust to suit your taste. At this point, you may need to add some water or, if you added too much water, you may need to keep heating it to absorb the extra fluid. It is done when it reaches a thick consistency and the dried fruit plumps. If you don't want chunky/homestyle applesauce, use a potato masher to break up the chunks. Cool and refrigerate. It can also be frozen and stored for weeks.
3. **Other optional ingredients**: sliced pears boiled along with the apples, diced dried apricots added with raisins and/or cranberries. Chopped nuts, walnuts, or pecans added at the end or to the cooled applesauce before serving are delicious, too!

MAC AND CHEESE
BRIAN FLEMING

So this is a recipe handed down in my family and it's a simple dish. I have used it several times, one of the best turn outs of it was at the firehouse on a drill night. I more than tripled the recipe to make two large trays, and well, they were licked clean by everyone that night.

Ingredients:

1 box elbow pasta
1½-2 cups whole milk
About 2 heaping spoons flour
Pam spray
2 spoons butter
1 spoon dry mustard
Bags of shredded sharp cheese works the best. I tend to add a jack cheese to add some heat. Other cheeses work well, too, but keep the base of cheddar

Directions:

1. In large saucepan spray Pam, melt butter, add flour & mustard, stir constantly.

2. Add milk, stir constantly.
3. When thickened, add cheeses. Stir frequently.
4. When melted, take off burner, add cooked pasta, stir. Put into casserole dish & sprinkle with more cheese & breadcrumbs.
5. Bake at 350 degrees about 1 hour until the top is a golden brown.

CORN FRITTERS

Ingredients:

1 egg
120 ml. whole milk
85 g plain flour
½ tsp. baking powder
145 g corn kernels, fresh or drained from a can
1 pinch salt and freshly ground pepper
4 tbsp. vegetable oil
4 poached eggs and 4 slices of lox (or smoked salmon), for serving

Directions:

1. Have your poached eggs and slices of lox or smoked salmon ready to go – the fritters don't take long.
2. In a medium bowl, whisk the egg and milk. Slowly add the flour and baking powder and whisk until smooth. Stir in the corn and season with salt and pepper.
3. Heat the oil in a cast-iron skillet over medium-high heat. Test if the oil is ready to fry by adding a small drop of batter into the oil. If it sizzles, it is ready.

4. Spoon about 60 ml./2 fl. oz. of the batter into the oil to form a round, 2 fritters in at a time.
5. Lightly fry on both sides until golden, about 2 minutes per side. Transfer to paper towels to drain. Repeat with the remaining batter.
6. Serve the corn fritters topped with lox and poached eggs.

ORANGE CAULIFLOWER: A VEGETARIAN VERSION OF THE POPULAR CHINESE ORANGE CHICKEN

Ingredients:

CRISPY CAULIFLOWER
1 head cauliflower
1 cup water
¾ cup flour
1 tbsp. garlic powder
¼ tsp. salt
2 cups panko breadcrumbs

ORANGE SAUCE
2 cups orange juice, fresh squeezed preferred
1 cup granulated sugar
4 tbsp. rice vinegar
4 tbsp. soy sauce
½ tsp. dried ground ginger
4 garlic cloves
2 tsp. Sriracha hot sauce
4 tbsp. cornstarch
½ cup water

Directions:

ROASTED CRISPY CAULIFLOWER

1. Preheat the oven to 400 degrees. Line a large baking sheet with parchment paper.
2. Wash and cut cauliflower into bite-sized pieces.
3. In a large bowl, add water, flour, garlic powder and salt. Whisk until well combined. Place the breadcrumbs in a medium sized bowl and set it next to the wet batter bowl. Also place your baking sheet nearby.
4. Add the cauliflower to the bowl with the wet batter and toss to combine, coating all the pieces well.
5. One by one, remove a cauliflower piece, tapping any excess batter off, and roll in the breadcrumbs to coat. Place on the prepared baking sheet and make sure they are not touching each other, or they will all get stuck together as they bake.
6. Bake for about 20-30 minutes until golden brown.

ORANGE SAUCE

1. In a large pan (large enough to fit the cauliflower and sauce), add all sauce ingredients except the cornstarch and water. Bring to a boil, and cook for a minute or two.
2. Mix the cornstarch and water in a small bowl to combine, and then add to the pot. Stir over medium-high heat constantly for a couple of minutes until the sauce thickens.

TO FINISH

1. Once the cauliflower is done, add it to the pan with the orange sauce and stir to coat. Serve over brown or white rice. Sprinkle with green onions and/or sesame seeds. Serve hot and enjoy!

FERMENTED GARLIC HONEY

Ingredients:

12 garlic cloves (about 1 head), crushed
1½ cups raw honey

Directions:

1. Place garlic in jar. Pour honey over garlic and stir to combine, making sure all the garlic gets coated.
2. Seal jar and let sit at room temperature 3 days.
3. Unscrew and remove lid to let out any gases; give garlic honey a stir. (You'll most likely see tiny bubbles at this stage, which means the fermentation process has started.)
4. Reseal jar and let sit, stirring once every other day, at least one week before using.

GOLDEN FAMILY CHOPPED STRING BEANS

A traditional recipe among Ukrainian and other Eastern European Jews, this chopped string beans recipe was made by Al and Elliott's mother, Rose, and served at almost every Golden family get together for over 50 years. It became such a tradition that Al's son Bradley still makes it today. Some people compare this recipe to a vegetarian version of chopped liver and it can be eaten on crackers and served as an appetizer or as a side dish.

Ingredients:

1 to 2 onions, chopped
2 tbsp. oil (or a little more if needed)
2 cans French cut string beans, chopped
1 hard-boiled egg, chopped
Wheat germ (about 2 tbsp.)
Mayonnaise (1 tsp., or just enough to hold ingredients together)
Walnuts (½ cup, chopped), optional

Directions:

1. Sauté onions in oil until soft and slightly golden in color. Let cool a little while.
2. Add 2 cans of French cut string beans to onions and oil mixture, then add the chopped hard-boiled egg and wheat germ.
3. If desired, add ½ cup of chopped walnuts.
4. Add mayonnaise and mix ingredients together.

PAN FRIED ASPARAGUS

Ingredients:

¼ cup butter
2 tbsp. olive oil
1 tsp. salt
¼ tsp. pepper
3 garlic cloves, minced
1 lb. asparagus

Directions:

In frying pan melt butter, add in olive oil, salt, pepper, and garlic. Cook for 1 minute. Add asparagus, cook approximately 10 minutes until desired crispiness is reached.

SQUASH AND ZUC

Ingredients:

4-6 pieces of bacon
2 squash
2 zucchini
⅓ cup of sugar
1 tbsp. of salt

Directions:

1. Chop up bacon and cook in skillet. Once it is almost cooked, add squash and zucchini. Add enough water to just cover.
2. Add sugar and salt then cover. Slowly bring to a boil.
3. Let boil for a few minutes then uncover and continue cooking until most of the water has evaporated or until vegetables are of the desired consistency.
4. Drain remaining water.

TWICE BAKED POTATOES

Ingredients:

4 large or 6 medium potatoes
4 tbsp. butter
⅓ cup sour cream
2 green onions or chives
½ cup cheddar cheese
Salt and pepper to taste

Directions:

1. Bake potatoes desired amount.
2. Cut tops off of potatoes.
3. Scoop out potatoes, leaving a thin layer over the skin for support.
4. In a bowl mash potatoes and add 2 tbsp. of butter plus ⅓ cup sour cream.
5. Add and stir in chives/green onions, cheese (use most of the cheese but leave some for sprinkling on top), salt, and pepper.
6. Sprinkle some cheese on top.

7. Pour 2 tbsp. of melted butter over the tops.
8. Add more salt and pepper on top.
9. Bake 20 minutes at 350 degrees.

BRAISED FRIED CABBAGE

Ingredients:

4 strips bacon, diced
2 garlic cloves
1 large onion, sliced
2 lbs. shredded cabbage
½ tsp. caraway seed (or less to taste)
½ cup chicken stock
½ cup dry white wine
Salt and pepper to taste

Directions:

1. Heat Dutch Oven.
2. Add bacon and sauté until crisp.
3. Add garlic and onion.
4. Sauté until clear.
5. Add cabbage, stock, and wine.
6. Cover and cook 5 minutes.
7. Remove lid and cook 15 minutes, stirring.
8. Season with caraway, salt, and pepper to taste.

RICE WITH RAISINS ~ PANAMANIAN STYLE

Ingredients:

1½ lbs. of rice (5 cups)
1 lb. (1 box) of raisins
2 tbsp. margarine (soup spoon)
4 cinnamon sticks (or 2 tsp. of cinnamon powder)
½ cup of honey (if there is no honey you can use the same amount of brown sugar)
3 tbsp. vegetable oil
Salt to taste

Directions:

1. In the cooking pot in which the rice will be cooked, margarine, raisins, cinnamon, and honey are placed with enough water to cover them. Cook in low heat until the raisins soften (they look almost round). It is important not to let the liquid dry out.
2. Once the raisins are cooked, rice, oil, water to cover the mixture, and salt to taste are added to the same cooking pot. Cook over medium heat until the excess water is boiled and the rice is visible.

3. When the excess water is boiled, cover cooking pot and cook on low heat until rice is cooked. At this point, stir to bring the rice at the bottom of the pot to the top. The rice at the bottom should still be wet. Place lid on pot again for another 4-6 minutes.
4. Stir again to bring the rice at the bottom of the pot to the top. At this point the rice should be fully cooked. In the event that it is not, the rice should be served hot as a side order.

Note: It is usually served with stewed chicken and salad.

CORN & CHEESE CASSEROLE

Ingredients:

2 bags frozen corn (large ones)
1 brick cream cheese
1 stick salted butter
1 bag mixed shredded cheese (whatever you like, I use a mix of cheddar and mozzarella)
1 cup of bacon crumbles (I get the bag at Costco) add more if you like extra bacon

Directions:

1. Put corn in microwave in oven-safe casserole dish, cover. Heat on high for 5 minutes, stir, then heat again for 10 minutes covered.
2. After corn is hot, mix in cream cheese & butter until the cream cheese and butter are melted and mixed well.
3. Add the shredded cheese and bacon, mix until well combined.
4. Put uncovered into preheated 350 degree oven for 30 minutes or until you see it bubbling.

POP ELGIN'S MASHED POTATOES

RUSSEL AVOLIO

This recipe was introduced to my family when I was about 5 or 6 years old. We moved into our family home after having returned from Lawton, Oklahoma, where my dad had been stationed for Field Artillery Training with the New York National Guard. Pop Elgin was our next door neighbor, and I had found out years later he was a Merchant Mariner-Engineer who served on liberty ships.

All of our new neighbors decided to have a Thanksgiving celebration, with each family bringing a dish to share. This was the dish Pop Elgin and his wife prepared for everyone. My mom and everyone else loved the recipe, and Pop Elgin was kind enough to share it.

It has since become a family tradition at Thanksgiving. Over the years, I don't often spend Thanksgiving with my side of the family, but this dish is now served when I celebrate the holiday with my in-laws and is now being shared with my Maritime family.

Ingredients:

5 lbs. potatoes
1 lb. bacon
1 tbsp. olive oil

3 tbsp. half & half
2 eggs, beaten
1 large yellow onion
1 brick Philadelphia Cream Cheese
1 stick salted butter
2 fire roasted red peppers
Salt and pepper

Directions:

1. Place a large pot of salted water on stove and bring to a boil.
2. Peel all potatoes, cut each in half, then cut each half in quarters; this is to allow for quicker cooking.
3. When water reaches a boil, add the potatoes and cook until soft. Potatoes are done when a fork inserted causes the potato to break easily. Be sure not to overcook. (Usually about 20 min. cooking time.)
4. While the potatoes are cooking, cook the bacon. The bacon should be cooked such that it is just lightly crispy.
5. When cooked, rough chop the bacon and set aside.
6. Slice the onion into thin slices. If you have, use a mandolin; it works best. Heat a pan on medium heat and add olive oil to hot pan. Do not let the olive oil smoke, it changes the flavor. Cook the onion, stirring periodically until soft and translucent. Set aside.
7. Chop the roasted red peppers. (You can make your own, but the jarred ones work fine, too.) Set aside.
8. When potatoes are done, reserve one cup of the cooking water and drain the potatoes. Return potatoes to the same pot, and use a potato masher or ricer to mash smooth.
9. Add the half & half, butter, salt and pepper to taste and mash the butter in until well combined.
10. Add the cream cheese and again mash/mix until combined. If the mixture appears a little thick, add the cooking water one tablespoon at a time until you reach your desired thickness. Don't make them watery, you want these to be a bit on the thick side.

11. Add the bacon, onions, red peppers and egg.
12. Mix until thoroughly combined. Place into a large Pyrex casserole dish. Place uncovered in oven preheated 350 degrees and cook until top is golden brown. (I typically make this a day ahead of time as the flavors mingle together the longer it sits. If you choose to do this, let the dish come up to room temp before putting into the oven to make sure it heats up evenly. If you go straight from fridge to oven, you can get uneven heating and will have cold spots.

CANLIS SALAD

CARL HAUSHEER ~ FROM SEATTLE LAKE UNION NEAR THE FISHING FLEETS

Ingredients:

2 heads of romaine, outer leaves discarded, chopped
4 bacon slices, chopped
1 cup cubed fresh Italian bread
1 egg
¼ cup freshly squeezed lemon juice
½ cup olive oil
Kosher salt and black pepper
½ cup scallions, thinly sliced
¾ cup fresh mint, roughly chopped
1 tbsp. fresh oregano leaves, roughly chopped
12 cherry tomatoes, halved
1 cup freshly grated Romano cheese

Directions:

1. Wash the lettuce in cold water, dry thoroughly, and put in the refrigerator to chill.
2. In a large pan set over medium-high heat, fry the bacon until it is nearly crisp, then remove to a bowl. Drain off all but one

tablespoon of fat, then add the bread cubes to the pan and toss to coat. Bring heat to low and toast, tossing the bread occasionally with a spoon until it is crisp. Remove to another bowl.
3. Make the dressing. Place a whole egg in its shell into a coffee cup, then pour boiling water over the top. Allow the egg to cook for 60 seconds, then remove it. Rinse with water until cool. In a mixing bowl, whisk together the lemon juice and olive oil, then crack the coddled egg into the bowl and whisk again, vigorously, to emulsify. Add salt and pepper to taste, then set aside.
4. In a salad bowl, combine cold lettuce, scallions, mint, oregano and the reserved bacon. Toss with enough dressing to coat the lettuce, then top with the tomatoes, the croutons and a goodly shower of cheese.

SAUTÉED SAUERKRAUT

Ingredients:

2 tbsp. brown sugar
1 tsp. caraway seeds or 3 to 4 whole cloves
1 tbsp. vinegar
¼ cup butter
½ cup sliced onion
3 lbs. sauerkraut (washed)

Directions:

1. Cover the pot and cook until kraut, butter, and onion is hot.
2. Add remaining ingredients and cook for 15 minutes.

PART FOUR
SAUCES AND MARINADES

CRANBERRY SAUCE

Ingredients:

1 bag (12 oz.) fresh cranberries
¾ cup sugar
1 tsp. lemon zest
1 cup water

Directions:

In a medium saucepan, combine cranberries, sugar, lemon zest, and water. Bring to a boil. Reduce to a simmer and cook until berries are soft. About 10 minutes.

If desired, add extra ingredients after cooking in a bowl. Let cook to room temperature.

SHISH-KA-BAB MARINADE

Ingredients:

½ cup oyster sauce
2 tbsp. oil
2 tbsp. soy sauce
1 clove garlic
2 scallions

Directions:

1. Mince garlic. Cut scallions in one-inch pieces.
2. Marinade meat (tender cuts of beef or lamb) at least 2 hours to overnight.

UGLY SAUCE

Ingredients:

½ cup grape jelly
½ cup chili sauce

Directions:

1. Mix the two together. As long as you use equal parts, you can adjust the size of the recipe.
2. Goes great with brown meatballs, meatloaf, burgers, etc.

DRY RIBS RUB

Ingredients:

2½ tbsp. paprika
2 tbsp. salt
2 tbsp. garlic powder
1 tbsp. fresh ground black pepper
1 tbsp. onion powder
1 tbsp. cayenne
1 tbsp. dried oregano
1 tbsp. dried thyme

Directions:

1. The rub mix will make ⅔ of a cup.
2. Scrub the ribs under cold water. Damp dry with paper towel. Sprinkle the rub on both sides of the ribs. Cook on low for 6-8 hours or until the tenderness you desire.
3. If you want BBQ sauce on them, add one hour before they are almost done.
4. All crock pots are different as far as heating temperature Mine is very hot on low and it only takes 6 hours.

DRY RIBS RUB

Ingredients:

2 cups brown sugar (light or dark)
½ cup paprika
⅓ cup garlic salt
2 tbsp. onion salt
2 tbsp. chili powder
1 tbsp. cayenne pepper
1 tbsp. black pepper
1½ tsp. dried oregano

PUTANESCA SAUCE

Ingredients:

3 tbsp. olive oil
3 cloves of garlic, mashed
1 small onion, diced
1 can (28 oz.) petite diced tomatoes
Anchovy paste or 3-4 anchovy filets
½ cup kalamata onions, coarsely chopped
2 tbsp. capers, finely chopped
Dried or fresh parsley, basil, oregano, red pepper flakes for seasoning, coarsely chopped

Directions:

1. In a large frying pan add anchovy and onion. Stir well.
2. Add garlic and stir until golden.
3. Add tomatoes and stir well.
4. Add spices (basil, red pepper, parsley, oregano) and stir well.
5. Add olives and capers. Stir well.

SURVIVING THE NIGHT SHIFT
MATTHEW BONVENTO, '01

Anyone who has been to sea can speak at length about the midnight meal, or *Midrats*. There are a number of other not so family friendly names that will not be mentioned here. You can use your imagination, or ask your nearest sailor.

Midrats consist of either the leftovers of some meal during the day or cold cuts. If you are lucky and it is early enough in the voyage, the cold cuts are still decent. The longer into the voyage you get, the more freezer burned and unappetizing they become. Little do landlubbers know how slimy cold cuts get as they age.

Bread is another story. If frozen properly and thawed properly, the low quality bread that the company bought does not taste too bad. If your steward is lazy or incompetent, that bread will either be mushy or hard as a rock.

What to put in between the bread is the most important decision. Those highly questionable cold cuts or peanut butter and jelly. PB&J is a staple. I lived off of that in a shipyard period for two months. That was lunch everyday, PB&J. Most ships will buy the generic grape jelly or strawberry jam. If you are lucky, you may see *Concord*. But peanut butter, that staple of all staples, is the debate . . . smooth or chunky? I have seen Suez Canal pilots fight over peanut butter and cigarettes. To the average person, this seems like an open and shut argument. Smooth wins, right? Sales of smooth peanut butter in the US exceed chunky. However, health nuts will debate the extra fiber in chunky peanut butter, thus making it healthier.

Before you next go to the store, ask yourself, what will sit better in your stomach at 0400? And you will know the gastronomical debate of being a mariner at sea!

PART FIVE
SOUP AND STEW
KEITH GIBNEY

In the following story, the names of all involved have been changed for the purposes of anonymity. That being said, the events in this story are non-fictitious and actually happened. To give you a full view of all the players involved in this event, I have to tell you one story to tell you another.

I was sailing as an AB (Able-Bodied Seaman) aboard the USNS Red Cloud, and with our load of cargo we were to navigate the Suez Canal to get it to its destination. Now, anyone who has sailed those waters knows that this is a very long trip and has to be taken in multiple stages. Along with these various different stages, every good journey needs a good guide (or in the case of this story, multiple canal pilots). This will play a key part in the story, but we'll circle back to that.

One of the mates that I was sailing with was a good ole boy from Tennessee. For the purposes of this story, we'll call him "Jimbo." Well, to put it mildly, the religious views and practices of the Middle East vary considerably from that of Western Civilization, more specifically, their necessity for prayer rugs and their proper placement or direction. I say this last part because where the channel pilot decided to place his prayer rug interfered with the "shipboard religion" (specifically the religion of coffee and its necessity, especially at 3:30 in the morning). So, the placement of the prayer rug was right in front of the coffee machine on the bridge. For anyone who is familiar with Middle Eastern religion, or religion of any culture for that matter, there are items of significant value. In this case, the prayer rug. So, the pilot had placed his rug, and Jimbo came up the bridge at 3:30 a.m. to prepare for the start of the 4:00 a.m. journey to the next staging point. I will point out that I was sitting on the bridge watching the following events unfold. The first thing Jimbo always did before his shift was to grab a cup of much needed coffee. So he shuffled up to the coffee machine . . . right across the prayer rug. I sat there waiting for "The Show" to begin, and begin it did. The pilot came unglued, shouting God knows what in his native tongue (which none of us spoke), and then there was some spitting and hand waving along with some elaborate and I'm sure unkind hand gestures. Jimbo just stood there (sipping his coffee) and waited for the pilot to get it all out of his system. When it appeared that the rant was complete, Jimbo responded in the driest, most sarcastic tone I have ever heard (truly, it was a thing of beauty). "Well, that's what you get for blocking my coffee, you dum sumbich!!!" (It's not a spelling error, trust me.) The pilot was obviously taken aback. He scooped up his prayer rug and stormed out to the port bridge wing. He pulled out a cell phone and started calling other pilots up the channel. I have no doubt that this one incident affected the events to come.

Now, anyone who has traveled in that part of the world is familiar with something called a "Baksheesh." For those of you who are not, it is a small sum of money (or, in this case, goods) given as a tip, bribe, or charitable donation. So, let me paint the scene for you. This colorful cast of characters include Captain "Beagle," Chiefmate "Barney" (as in Fife), Jimbo, and me. Now, because of the incident previously stated, every pilot that we picked up along the way (and dropped off) requested an abnormally large and bizarre list of items. One pilot requested two jars of peanut butter, another requested a case of coffee. The pilot that caused the most stir demanded three cases of menthol filtered cigarettes from the slop chest (ship's store), a pair of coveralls, and one of the SIU Zippo lighters. Finally the "Beagle" had had enough and advised "Barney" to send him packing without so much as a thank you. While a Baksheesh is customary, extortion is not. His replacement was the main focus of the story. This guy was just happy to get on the ship ... Here's why.

When a pilot is picked up, the pilot boat comes up along the starboard side of the vessel to come aboard. In the case of a vessel as large as the Red Cloud, a Jacob's ladder (rope ladder) is required. Now, before I go into this next part of the story, you must understand that in the Suez canal, there is all types of marine life, and it gets stirred up when the vessels come through. In the case of this story, the wildlife in question was sand sharks. So, I was on the bridge at the helm and "Beagle" was calling out navigational commands. Barney had been sent to collect this new pilot, and Jimbo was verifying course and handling communications. The call came across the radio advising of the pilot boat coming along side. The following radio communication (and I can't emphasize enough) actually happened, verbatim.

"Pilot boat in position!" Barney reported. "Pilot is at ladder" ... 'Pilot is climbing ladder" ... "Pilot is frozen on the ladder" ... "Pilot is in the water!!!" ... "Pilot is back on the ladder!!!" ... "Pilot is rapidly climbing the ladder" ... "Pilot is onboard ... Finally!"

If you are confused with what had just happened, the young and inexperienced pilot had gotten halfway up the Jacob's ladder (about 25ft up) and suddenly developed a fear of heights. In pausing out of his fear of heights, his hands slipped from the rungs of the ladder causing him to fall 30 feet into the water below ... right into a nest of sand sharks that had been disturbed by the presence of the pilot boat. Realizing that he was in a nest of angry (and potentially hungry) sand sharks, suddenly his fear of heights seemed of little importance. The pilot frantically scrambled back aboard the pilot boat. He then closed his eyes and with all the gracefulness of a newborn giraffe, climbed expeditiously up the Jacob's ladder to meet Barney, who was waiting for him at the top of the ladder.

Apparently, on the way to the bridge, they stopped by the slop chest to get the pilot a dry set of clothes because when he arrived on the bridge, he was dressed in full ship attire. I will say that he was the most respectful of the pilots that we had met that day, and I'm sure that providing him with a dry change of clothes might have something to do with that. The rest of the voyage was fairly uneventful, but after the days events, I was ok with a little normalcy. All in all, it was the most entertaining channel navigation that I have ever been a part of.

LENTIL STEW

Ingredients:

½ cup fresh chopped cilantro (coriander), divided
3 carrots
3 celery stalks, including leaves
2 tbsp. extra virgin olive oil
1 large onion, diced
1 clove garlic, crushed
2 cups dry red lentils
¼ cup pearl barley (omit for GF)
2 quarts vegetable or chicken stock
1½ tsp. cumin
1 tsp. hyssop or parsley
½ tsp. sumac (optional)
1 bay leaf
Salt and pepper to taste

Directions:

1. Roughly chop the cilantro. Scrub the carrots, then cut them into

chunks (do not peel). Cut celery into chunks, including leaves. Reserve.
2. In a medium sized soup pot, heat olive oil over medium heat. Add diced onion and sauté until translucent.
3. Add garlic, carrot chunks, and celery. Continue to sauté till onion turns golden and ingredients begin to caramelize. Add red lentils and barley to the pot, stir. Cover mixture with 2 qts. of broth and bring to a boil. Reduce heat to a simmer. Add ¼ cup of the fresh cilantro to the pot along with the cumin, hyssop or parsley, sumac (optional) and bay leaf; stir.
4. Cover the pot and let the stew simmer slowly for 1½ to 2 hours, stirring every 30 minutes, until barley is tender and the stew is thickened. Garnish soup with remaining cilantro.

Gluten Free Modification: Omit the barley for a more soup-like texture, or substitute ¼ cup brown rice for the barley. Rice is not a Biblical-era grain, but it makes a delicious substitute for those struggling with Celiac or gluten intolerance.

CREAM OF PEANUT SOUP

Ingredients:

1 medium onion, chopped
2 stalks celery, chopped
¼ cup butter
2 cups peanut butter, smooth
3 tbsp. all purpose flour
2 quarts chicken stock
1¾ cup light cream
⅓ cup chopped peanuts

Directions:

1. Sauté onion and celery in butter until soft but not brown. Stir in flour until well blended.
2. Add chicken stock, stirring constantly until boiling. Remove from heat and rub through a sieve (if not available, don't worry, the soup will be slightly chunky).
3. Add peanut butter and cream, stir in until well blended.
4. Return to low heat, but do not boil.
5. Soup may be served warm or cold.

CHEDDAR BROCCOLI SOUP

Ingredients:

3 tbsp. butter
1 small onion, chopped
2 tbsp. all purpose flour
1 cup half-and-half
1½ cups chicken broth
2 cups chopped broccoli
1 carrot, chopped
1 celery stalk, chopped
1¼ cup shredded cheddar cheese
Salt and pepper to taste

Directions:

1. Melt butter in a stock pot over medium-high heat; add onion and sauté until tender, 3 to 4 minutes. Whisk in flour and continue to stir until mixture turns golden brown, about 5 minutes. Slowly add half-and-half to onion mixture, stirring until mixture is smooth. Add chicken broth; season with salt and ground black pepper.

2. Reduce heat to medium-low and simmer mixture until thickened, about 10 minutes. Add broccoli, carrot, and celery. Simmer until vegetables are tender yet crisp, about 20 minutes.
3. Reduce heat to low. Add cheddar cheese to soup and cook, stirring occasionally, until cheese melts, about 5 minutes.

CLAM CHOWDER

Ingredients:

2 yellow onions, medium-large
1 celery stalk
4 potatoes, medium
1 can clams with juice (3 lbs. 3 oz.)
½ lb. butter
3 qts. milk (room temperature)
Flour
Chicken base
Salt
Ground oregano
Garlic powder
White pepper
Old Bay (optional)

Directions:

1. Dice potatoes into small pieces.
2. Chop celery and onion into small-medium pieces and add to pot with potatoes and a touch of all the seasonings (oregano,

garlic power, white pepper, old bay). Cook until potatoes are almost soft, periodically stirring.
3. Combine 2 tbsp. each of chicken base, oregano, garlic power, white pepper, old bay, and all the butter to make rue.
4. Add flour to rue and bring to a slow boil, continuously stirring for a few minutes until flour is cooked out.
5. Add clams and juice to rue.
6. Slowly add milk to rue when mixture starts to thicken. Add slowly and steadily.
7. Combine celery mixture to rue, stirring occasionally.
8. Salt to taste.
9. Add clams and let simmer for 1 to 1½ hours.

HAMBURGER BARLEY VEGETABLE SOUP

Ingredients:

1½ lbs. ground beef
6 cups water
3 beef bouillon cubes or packets
2 cups sliced carrots
1½ cups coarsely chopped celery
1½ cups coarsely chopped onion
2 8 oz. can of diced tomatoes, undrained
1 8 oz. can of tomato sauce
1 cup uncooked barley
1 tsp. salt
2 bay leaves

Directions:

Place in large crockpot on high for 3 to 4 hours.

INSTANT POT CHICKEN SOUP

Ingredients:

2 large chicken breasts
Roasted garlic and herb spices
One cup chicken broth
For the soup:
3 cartons of chicken broth or stock
1 tbsp. of EVOO
1 tbsp. of diced garlic
1 large onion, diced
5 cups of carrots, diced or sliced (depending on liking)
5 cups of celery, diced or sliced (depending on liking)
Italian spices

Directions:

1. In an Instant Pot, pour one cup chicken broth on the trivet. Place the chicken breast and put the roasted garlic and herb spices over the chicken breast to taste. Place the instant pot to manual pressure and set to 15 minutes. Once done, allow for natural release.

2. Take chicken out and save the liquid.
3. Turn Instant Pot to sauté mode. Once hot, put the EVOO in and cook the onion until translucent. Add garlic. After a minute or two, add the carrots and celery. Sauté for 2 to 3 minutes. Then add the broth up to the max fill line (include the broth from steaming the chicken). Add Italian spices to liking, cover, set to manual and cook for 5 minutes, with a natural release for 10 minutes.
4. While the vegetables are cooking, use two forks to shred the chicken. Once the Instant Pot is released, add the chicken to the soup, stir, and let the chicken heat up in the soup, then serve.

EGG DROP SOUP

Ingredients:

1 cup of sweet corn (frozen or fresh)
3-4 eggs
2 tbsp. sesame oil
Corn starch
2 cups water
2 cups chicken broth

Directions:

Bring water, corn, and broth to a rolling boil. Beat the eggs and then whisk into boiling liquid. Add sesame oil to taste and corn starch for thickness.

BEAN AND PASTA SOUP
(PASTA E FAGIOLI)

Ingredients;

½ cup onion, minced
¼ cup olive oil
1 cup sliced celery
6 cup chicken broth
½ tsp. salt
¼ tsp. pepper
1¼ cup tubular pasta, cooked
4 cups canned white or red kidney beans or northern beans, drained
3-4 spare ribs or two thin shoulder pork chops or a ham bone
Parmesan cheese
Parsley for garnish

Directions:

1. Sauté onion in the olive oil until golden (no longer) in a Dutch Oven.
2. Add celery and pork and cook over low heat, stirring occasionally for about 10 minutes.
3. Add all except the pasta, beans, and parmesan.

4. Cover the pot and cook for 30 minutes.
5. Add the pasta and beans and cook an additional 5 minutes.
6. Let stand for five more minutes, then add more chicken broth to barely cover the pasta and beans.
7. Stir in cheese and sprinkle with snipped parsley, if desired.
8. Pork may be cut up and added or saved for another meal.

CHIOPPINO ITALIAN FISHERMAN'S SOUP

JEFFREY PERLSTEIN

I grew up in Monsey, New York. On Sunday, we would get the *New York Times*, and I would go through the cooking section looking for interesting recipes. My dad was a New York City police sergeant and a brilliant cook. On occasion, I would find a recipe that spoke to me and said "this will be outstanding," and my dad needed no further urging to cook it. This is one of those recipes:

Ingredients:

⅓ cup olive oil
1 cup chopped onion
1 cup chopped green onion
1 cup chopped green pepper
3 cloves garlic, crushed
1 dozen fresh little neck clams
1 large can tomatoes (1 lb. 12 oz.)
1 can tomato sauce (8 oz.)
1 cup dry red wine
¼ cup parsley chopped
2 tsp. kosher or coarse ground salt.
¼ tsp. ground pepper

¼ tsp. dried bay leaves
½ tsp. dried oregano
2 lb. mixed fresh fish: (a fish with a firm flesh) cod, halibut, grouper, etc
½ lb. shell fish: shrimp, rock lobster tail

Directions:

1. Heat oil in 6 quart dutch oven. Sauté onion, green onion, green pepper and garlic. Stirring occasionally until golden brown, about 10 minutes.
2. Open clams, reserve juice, and set clams aside.
3. To sautéed vegetables add: clam juice, tomatoes, tomato sauce, wine, parsley, salt, pepper, oregano, basil, one cup water. Bring to boil.
4. Reduce heat and simmer 30 minutes. Rinse fish, cut into large pieces.
5. Add fish, shrimp, clams. Return to just boiling. Reduce heat and simmer 15 minutes. Serve with hot crusty Italian bread.

NORWEGIAN LAPSKAUS
A HEARTY AND DELICIOUS STEW PERFECT FOR COLD WINTER EVENINGS

Ingredients:

5 lbs. potatoes, peeled and cubed
8 long carrots, peeled and cut into one inch pieces
2 onions, peeled and chopped
2 cans Libby's Corned Beef (must be Libby's) removed from can and diced
Salt and pepper to taste

Directions:

1. In a large pot add potatoes, carrots, and onions. Just covered with water to the level of ingredients and boil gently until tender. Remove from heat (don't drain remaining water).
2. Mash with a potato masher allowing for a chunky mixture. Then mash in corned beef until evenly distributed. Mixture should be stew like and not watery.
3. Serve with crisp bread and butter.

CHICKEN SOUSE – A BAHAMIAN CLASSIC

Ingredients:

2 onions
10 cloves
3 bay leaves
Chicken (wings only, or thighs only, entire chicken separated, cook's preference)
Russet/red potatoes
Whole corn on the cob
Carrots
6 limes (called sour in Bahama)
Salt (add to taste)
1 habanero (goat) pepper

Directions:

1. Quarter potatoes.
2. Slice onions into ¼ inch rings and then cut in half.
3. Slice limes in half.
4. Peel carrots and cut into roughly inch-long pieces.
5. Take chicken wings, thighs, breast, etc and clean them (see note)[1]
6. Marinate for several hours, up to a day.
7. In a large soup pot, add vegetables, chicken, cloves, and bay leaves.
8. Juice 6 limes into the pot then fill with water and a dime-sized amount of salt
9. Boil for one hour and ensure that a fork can be inserted into potatoes and come out clean.
10. Add more lime and salt as desired.
11. Add a pinch of habanero pepper to your bowl.

Note:

When I say clean the chicken, I mean to use lime and salt as a cleaning agent and wash the chicken thoroughly at least two times. The process is similar to washing a child's hands - you rinse with water first, hold their hands away from the water, lather thoroughly while vigorously scrubbing with your hands, then rinse & repeat the steps. This is what I mean by "cleaning the chicken." Only lime and abrasive granules of salt should be used instead of soap. After the chicken is "cleaned," a marinating solution should be used and the chicken should rest for a few hours to soak up the good stuff.

Cleaning the chicken is a Caribbean thing – you go to the store and once the bulk chicken is bought, it is all cleaned prior to being marinated and rests for at least 24 hours before being used in various portions to be cooked throughout the week. Sometimes stores pump the chicken with water to make it appear plumper – once the salt solution is left on the chicken, the osmosis allows you to see what you're truly dealing with, and the cleaning allows you to get rid of the film of blood and other unseen debris on the meat. It works!

SKIPPERHUSET'S FISH CHOWDER

When my dad Captain Leif N. W. Larsen retired from the marine industry, they started a Bed and Board in Norway in the house that had housed five generations of seafarers, including myself. As there is no restaurant on the island, they served dinner to the guests. This became one of the signature staples.

Fish Stock:

2 liters (quarts) water
Green part of 1 leek
1 carrot
Parsley stalks

A little peel or greens from celeriac
1 bay leaf
1 horseradish leaf (optional)
10 black peppercorns
2 kilo (4½ lb) small coley or other white fish

Vegetables:

1 carrot
1 potato
1 small leek
1½ kg. (3 lb.) haddock or cod
1¼ dl. (½ cup) chopped chives

Soup:

35 g (2 tbsp.) butter
35 g (¼ cup) all-purpose flour
7½ dl. (3 cups) boiling fish stock
2½ dl. (1 cup) whole milk
1 dl. (½ cup) whipping cream

1. The secret with this and any fish soup is the fish stock, butter, cream, and fresh fish, plus lots of chives.
2. Place all the ingredients for the stock, except the fish, in the stock pot and bring water to a boil. Simmer while cleaning the fish.
3. Clean and scale the fish. Remove the eyes and gills. Use a fish brush along the backbone to remove any membrane and blood. Following these steps helps to keep the stock clear.
4. Cut the fish into pieces and add to the vegetable stock. Lower the heat and simmer for 25 minutes, skimming regularly. Strain. (This can be made ahead and frozen.)

Vegetables and Fish:

1. Wash and peel the vegetables. Dice the carrot and potatoes then slice the leeks.
2. Clean and fillet the fish. Cut the fish into 4 pieces of equal size.
3. Cook the vegetables and fish separately in lightly salted water until just tender, about 5 minutes.

Soup:

1. Make roux by melting the butter and stir in the flour. Let sizzle for about 30 seconds, stirring constantly.
2. Whisk in the liquid (fish stock, milk, and cream). Simmer for 15 minutes, stirring constantly.
3. Just before serving, stir the vegetables into the soup.
4. To serve, pour the soup into bowls (preferably warmed). Top with fish. Sprinkle 2 tablespoons of finely chopped chives over each bowl to form a green layer over the soup.

CHICKEN SOUP

CARL HAUSHEER

When I was a captain of the old bell boat tankers like the John Tabling, there was an oil burning stove in the galley that would make perfect slow cooking meals. Soup was always on, and good cooking smells would have everyone gather in the galley. Shipyard workers who would not mind fixing a few things, as they liked the soup on a cold winter day. You can roast a few chickens and use leftovers or use a whole chicken uncooked.

Ingredients:

1 (3 pound) whole chicken
4 carrots, halved
4 stalks celery, halved
1 large onion, chopped fine
Leeks chopped fine
Water to cover
Salt and pepper to taste
1 tsp. chicken bouillon granules or stock

Directions:

1. Put the chicken, carrots, celery and onion in a large soup pot and cover with cold water. Heat and simmer, uncovered, until the chicken meat falls off of the bones. (Skim off foam every so often.)
2. Take everything out of the pot. Strain the broth.
3. Pick the meat off of the bones and chop the carrots, celery and onion.
4. Season the broth with salt, pepper, and chicken bouillon to taste, if desired.
5. Return the chicken, carrots, celery and onion to the pot, stir together, and serve.

MATZAH BALL AND CHICKEN SOUP

Soup Ingredients:

4 cartons of either College Inn or Swanson chicken broth
1 whole cut up chicken
1 whole onion
5 carrots (2 cut-up in bite size pieces and 3 left whole)
5 parsnips (2 cut-up in bite size pieces and 3 left whole)
4 stalks of celery cut into thin slices
Bunch of fresh parsley
Bunch of fresh dill
Salt and pepper to taste

Matzah Ball recipe:

1 box of Streit's or Manischevitz Matzah Ball mix

Directions for Soup:

1. Place all of the chicken broth in a large stock pot.
2. Clean chicken and put into pot with broth.
3. Add all of the other ingredients ending with the salt and pepper and the parsley and dill on top.
4. Simmer on a low light for ½ hours.
5. Remove the onion, the 3 whole carrots, and the 3 whole parsnips. Place in a blender with 1 cup of the finished chicken soup. Blend until well blended and pulverized. Remove the parsley and dill and discard. Pour the carrots, parsnip, and chicken soup from the blender into the soup and mix it around.
6. When the soup and chicken are cold, remove chicken, cut it up into pieces and put back in soup.

Matzah balls:

1. Follow the recipe on the back of the box of the mix.
2. I cook them in salted water. When they are cooked according to the recipe on the box, place them into the soup.

FAT KID PARTY

"We're going to have a fat kid party today!" the AB exclaimed way too loudly at a time way too early, as everyone began to stumble toward the galley for coffee. The whole crew was exhausted from taking on fuel all night, and even the threat of copious amounts of delicious breakfast food was not enough to justify that sort of energy on that little sleep.

The tug's normal crew of four had been together for a what felt like longer than many marriages, and they had become like family. A new mate-in-training had recently joined the boat, and while he was nice enough, he was slightly out of place and struggled to find his place in the family dynamic.

As the mate-in-training pulled the tug away from the dock, the scent of breakfast filled the air from the lower decks to the wheelhouse. There was no question that the AB was hard at work in the galley. Just as the tug nosed into the ship she was to sail, the fire alarm went off . . . though it was nearly inaudible due to the shriek-like screams of "FIRE! FIRE!" from below. The mate-in-training jumped out of his seat as the captain's hand raised, signaling for him to stay at the controls. "Trust me, it's nothing. I'll go make sure."

As the captain reached to bottom of the stairs and entered the galley, the engineer leaned against the wall, scratching his head. He was an old, laid-back career sailor with not a care in the world, and he was obviously amused as the regular mate continued jumping and screaming, "Oh my god! FIRE!" The captain's face was curiously stoic as the engineer smiled and shrugged. Then the captain's gaze moved to the AB.

"Baking soda?!" The AB asked frantically as the flames grew bigger.

"Uh, yeah," the captain calmly affirmed with a nod. Before the captain could say any more, the fire was out and the AB and stove were both covered in baking soda. "Don't worry about breakfast," the captain laughed. "I'll order breakfast burritos when we get back to the dock. But get this cleaned up quick . . . I don't want our new friend seeing it and reporting it to the office!"

As the captain returned to the bridge, the mate-in-training was already asking questions about what had happened downstairs and was half way out of the chair and heading toward the stairs to go see. "Nothing to see!" The captain reassured. "Just a fire drill they were doing. Hey! You've only driven light boat . . . Sit back down! Want to work your first job?" The offer had been long awaited and was enough to cure the mate-in-training's curiosity. His face lit up as he quickly returned to the chair. "By the way, we decided to get breakfast burritos after we sail this ship, so be deciding what you want."

And that was the day that the AB learned how to use baking soda and the mate-in-training got to work his first job.

PART SIX
DINNER

PART SIX
THINGS

WHAHAPPEN TO OLD BAY
KEITH GIBNEY

WhaHappen to Old Bay

Back in 2006, I was stationed aboard the Soderman working as an A/B (Able-Bodied Seaman) and we were prepositioned in the middle of the Indian Ocean. We'll call it D Gar for the purposes of this story. On this particular voyage, I was having a conversation with our chief steward, Miss Georgia (chief steward being head of the Steward Dept.). We were discussing my fondness for ham salad and how it had been such a long time since I had someone who knew how to prepare it properly. This of course elicited the question, "Prepared Properly?" I explained that every time that I had requested it to be prepared, the cook would always use "Old Bay" seasoning, (a common staple in the maritime industry and used quite frequently in this particular cook's menu). The chief cook, we'll call him Moe, used to repeat an expression almost as much as he used Old Bay seasoning in his cooking. It is an expression that even to this day, makes me cringe... "Whahappen?!?" (This expression plays a definite part in the story.)

So, per my request, Miss Georgia instructed Moe to prepare ham salad the following day with the specific instructions not to use Old Bay seasoning. I believe the exact phrase that was used was "If I find out that you have used Old Bay in the preparation of this dish, so help me, I will take your entire stash of Old Bay and toss it off the stern. That way, the only creatures that will taste it will be the critters swimming in the lagoon!" She made Moe confirm that he understood the stipulations and the consequences if he ignored them.

The next day during the lunch hour, I excitedly rushed down to the mess (dining hall) and ordered ham salad. That excitement quickly turned to disgust after taking my first (and only) bite of this lunchtime concoction. I tasted one thing... Old Bay... Ugh! I took the plate to Miss Georgia, who was sitting down to coffee, and politely asked her to try a sample. Her reaction and response still makes me chuckle to this very day. She took one bite of this creation, and her face almost turned inside out. There was so much Old Bay that it sucked almost all of the moisture out of her mouth. In her thick southern accent, she said, "Son Of A Bitch!!!" (Add a southern accent, it'll make you laugh, too.) Well, the next thing that you heard was screaming, hollering and banging as Miss Georgia went to "Have a Discussion" with Moe... Then you see Miss Georgia marching to the stern with literally a case of Old Bay seasoning under each arm, and Moe chasing after her exclaiming, "WhaHappen? WhaHappen? WhaHappen?!?" She tossed both cases of Old Bay into the lagoon and without missing a beat turned to Moe and said "Say WhaHappen to me one more time!!!" I never did get my ham salad, but I got a great story out of it.

Now, I told you that story to tell you this one. On the island, there was a print shop that made custom t-shirts and they were able to use various different popular graphics in the printing of whatever you wanted. In my case, I chose Psycho Chihuahua. For those of you who are not familiar with this particular graphic, it was a cartoon chihuahua that was baring his teeth and you could insert a custom message for the scenario that you were trying to emphasize. (Google the image if you're not familiar with it.) Anyway, the custom message that I asked to be printed was the Psycho Chihuahua grinding his teeth and saying. "Say WhaHappen one more time!!!" I also had them include a graphic of a small can of Old Bay seasoning in the background. I presented Miss Georgia with the one-of-a-kind gift, and we have been friends ever since.

HOMESTYLE PUERTO RICAN RED BEANS

This recipe is served best with white rice and a non-fish protein of your choice (steak, pork chops, chicken). This recipe can also accompany yellow rice (as long as there are no beans in the yellow rice).

Serves 2-3 people depending on how much each person wants.

Ingredients (per 15 oz. can of red beans used):

1¼ cups water
1 large russet potato or (2) medium russet potatoes, peeled and cut into small cubes
1 7 oz. ham steak, cut into small cubes
1 cup pumpkin meat, cut into small cubes
1 8 oz. can Goya Spanish Tomato Sauce, Spanish Style
2 envelopes Sazon Without Annatto (white and orange box)
1 Knorr chicken boullion cube
1 can Goya Red Kidney Beans
Extra Virgin Olive Oil (two turns of the saucepan)

Veggies (place in a chopper to create a puree – we call this "Sofrito"):

2 garlic cloves
¼ green pepper
¼ red pepper
½ small yellow onion
¼ bunch cilantro
¼ medium tomato

Directions:

1. Place all of the ingredients into a medium saucepan (except the beans) and mix well.
2. Bring contents to a boil. Once boiling, leave contents boiling for 5 minutes.
3. As the sauce is prepping to boil, rinse the beans well in a strainer under water.
4. After 5 minutes of boiling, add the rinsed beans to the saucepan and mix well. Lower the heat to a simmer.
5. Set timer for 40 minutes. Stir the pot every 10 minutes until the timer lets you know you are done. Sauce will thicken as it cooks.
6. Serve on the side with your rice of choice.
7. Enjoy!

TIP:

This typical meal (rice, beans, protein) is served with a side of either ripe sweet plantains (maduros) or salty fried plantains (platanos). Either side can be made fresh if you have the green or ripe plantains handy, or you can find them in the freezer section of the supermarket (look for the Spanish frozen food section).

- Frozen maduros are already prepared and can be reheated in the microwave for quick and easy serving once the full meal is ready to eat. They give you the sweet to eat with the savory all on one plate.
- Frozen platanos are half prepared, so they need to be fried again to eat. You would begin frying them when the beans are

halfway cooked. Once fried, sprinkle some salt right away onto them. They give you the salty to eat with the savory all on one plate.

HOMESTYLE PUERTO RICAN POLLO GUISADO
(CHICKEN STEW)

This recipe is served best with white rice.

Serves 2-3 people depending on how much each person wants.

Ingredients:

1 big green pepper
1 big red pepper
1 large white onion
2 tomatoes
5 cloves garlic
Cilantro
5 small round potatoes
15 or less Goya Olives (with the pits)
A whole chicken cut up
Lemon juice
¼ cup Olive oil (Goya Virgin Olive Oil is the best)
1 Knorr chicken bouillon cubes
4 Goya Sazon packets (orange & white box without Annatto)
1 Goya Sazon packet (orange & yellow box with Azafran)
1 can tomato sauce (Goya is best tomato sauce)
Optional: 2 or 3 carrots (cut in round pieces - add after 1 hr cooking)

Optional: 2 corn on the cob (cut in 4 thin pieces each – to be added with potatoes)

Directions:

1. Cut peppers in long strips.
2. Cut onion in round slices.
3. Cut tomatoes in 1/8^{ths} the long way.
4. Cut garlic in thin slices the long way.
5. Cut cilantro leaves.
6. Rinse olives and put in a cup in cold water until you are ready to put them in (takes out the salt).
7. Wash chicken with lemon juice.
8. Rewash chicken again with plain water to take the lemon off.
9. Add water in pot to cover the bottom. (Make sure pot is big enough to place chicken pieces at bottom.)
10. Add olive oil and the bouillon cube. Shred it and spread all around.
11. Spread two packets of Goza Sazon.
12. Place chicken pieces all around the pot.
13. Peel and add potatoes, placing them in the center and around the chicken.
14. Add peppers, onions, tomatoes, olives, cilantro, garlic (spreading them all around).
15. Spread the remaining Goza Sazon packets around.
16. Open the tomato sauce and spread all around the chicken.
17. Add water in the can and mix to take up all the extra tomato and spread it around.
18. Cover pot, use low flame so that it cooks slowly and simmers.
19. After hour and a half, uncover pot and move chicken to make sure it's not sticking to bottom and taste the broth. According to your taste, you can add another packet of Goza Sazon (without Annatto) and/or ½ chicken bullion.
20. Cover for another hour, still in low flame, checking every ½ hour to make sure chicken is done.
21. Use your judgment on the cooking. Make sure that you don't have too much water. When done, the broth should be on the

thick side, not liquidy, and that the chicken is not overcooked so that it doesn't break apart.

Optional used for dressing up the Chicken:

- You can add the corn on the cob at the time you add the potatoes, OR
- In place of corn on the cob, a can of peas and carrots can be used which can be added about ½ hour before chicken is fully cooked.

TIP:

This typical meal is served with a side of either ripe sweet plantains (maduros) or salty fried plantains (platanos). Either side can be made fresh if you have the green or ripe plantains handy, or you can find them in the freezer section of the supermarket (look for the Spanish frozen food section).

- Frozen maduros are already prepared and can be reheated in the microwave for quick and easy serving once the full meal is ready to eat. They give you the sweet to eat with the savory all on one plate.
- Frozen platanos are half prepared, so they need to be fried again to eat. You would begin frying them when the beans are halfway cooked. Once fried, sprinkle some salt right away onto them. They give you the salty to eat with the savory all on one plate.

MELLA'S MEATBALLS
LILIANNA DI GESU

My Sicilian grandmother, Carmela Celestina Maccaronio Di Gesu, has a meatball recipe that can probably put that of your Nonna's to shame. It was passed down to her daughters-in-law, who have gone to great pains to replicate it.

I recall a period of time in my childhood when my mother's meatballs weren't coming out quite like Grandma's, and a dark cloud of despair seemed to hang over our dinner table when Mom's meatballs came out too hard, too soft, too bland, or just not enough like Grandma's.

Once Mom had mastered and re-mastered the Art of the Meatball several times over, the sun seemed to shine again, and all was right with the world. Meatballs, marinara, and pasta comprise the three main food groups consumed in my home, and the taste of home is what I miss most when I'm at sea. "Italian Night" on the T.S. Empire State simply does not cut it for me.

Ingredients:

2 pounds of ground beef or meatloaf mix (beef, veal, and pork)
3 slices of white bread or stale Italian bread, soaked in milk
⅓ cup grated parmesan romano cheese

1 tsp. garlic powder
1 tsp. dried basil
2 tsp. salt
½ tsp. fresh ground black pepper

Directions:

1. Soak bread in just enough milk to soften it so it can be mushed. Do not saturate it.
2. Combine meat and soaked bread in a large bowl, roughly mix it with your hands.
3. Add the rest of dry ingredients directly to meat/bread mix.
4. Combine to a consistency where meat is not sticky but is still able to be formed into a meatball. If it is sticky, add some bread crumbs. Be careful not to overmix as it will toughen the meat.
5. Take a palm sized ball of the meat (roughly ¼ cup), roll into meatball using hands. If the dough sticks to your hands, wet your hands with water.
6. Put meat on parchment paper-covered cookie sheet, evenly spaced but not too close together.
7. Bake in oven at 350 degrees for 15-20 minutes.
8. Remove from oven, transfer the meatballs to a pot of homemade marinara (**FOR THE LOVE OF ALL THAT IS HOLY, NOT RAGU OR PREGO**) where they will finish cooking.

ZWIEBELKUCHEN
(GERMAN ONION PIE)

This is me with my family on the day I departed for my 1/C cruise on Summer Sea Term 2019. My dad, Andrew, my sister, Juliet, and my mom, Elizabeth. I graduated from Fort Schuyler on July 24, 2020, with a degree in Marine Transportation and a USCG Third Mate's Unlimited Tonnage License.

For the crust:

1½ cups all purpose flour
½ tsp. salt
4 tbsp. butter at room temperature and cut into small pieces
¼ cup plus 1 tbsp. warm milk
1 package yeast
(It is perfectly acceptable to use a store bought or homemade pie crust instead of yeast dough.)

For the filling:

2 tbsp. butter
2 ¼ lbs. yellow onions, finely diced
5 slices thick cut bacon, finely sliced
1½ cups full fat sour cream
4 large eggs or 3 extra large
2 tbsp. all-purpose flour
2 tbsp. salt
1 tsp. caraway seed
Freshly ground black better

Start by making the dough:

Dissolve yeast in warm milk and let stand for 6 minutes. Place flour and salt in a food processor and make a well in the center. Add the butter and pour the milk mixture over. Using a dough hook, knead the dough on the "bread" setting for about 6 minutes. Add more milk (warm) or flour as needed. Form the dough into a ball, spray the dough ball with olive oil, cover loosely with plastic wrap, and let dough rise in a warm place until nearly doubled in size.

Onion/Bacon mixture:

Fry up the bacon. When bacon is done, add onions with 2 tbsp. of butter. Reduce heat and let the onions slowly caramelize to a nice golden brown, about 30-40 minutes, and allow mixture to cool.

To make the filling:

In a bowl, combine 1½ cups sour cream, eggs, 2 tbsp. flour, 2 tbsp. salt, 1 tsp. caraway seeds, and some freshly ground pepper. Add the Onion/Bacon mixture and combine thoroughly.

In a springform 9 inch dish, spread dough or pie crust on the bottom and up the sides. If using dough, place mixture in to reduce the retraction. Once the mixture is in, sprinkle the top with a few caraway seeds and put in the oven.

Bake in an oven preheated to 400 degrees for 55 to 60 minutes, until the top is light brown and center is fairly firm to the touch. Allow to cool for 2 minutes before serving.

CHILI

Ingredients:

4 regular size cans of black beans with sauce
8 packs of chili powder
4 chopped onions for flavor
½ a bulb of garlic
1 chopped green bell pepper for flavor
1 chopped red bell pepper for flavor
1 chopped banana pepper for flavor
2 small cans of green chili peppers for flavor
1 can tomato sauce (amount depends on consistency of chili)
1 can of tomato paste
4 chopped tomatoes
Crushed red pepper for heat
2 chopped jalapeño peppers for spice
3 pounds of cooked and drained hamburger meat

Directions:

Place combined ingredients in a large crock pot and cook on low heat for 24 hours. The slow cooking of all the peppers, onions, etc. is what gives it the flavor.

COUNTRY FRIED STEAK

Ingredients:

5 tbsp. all purpose flour
¼ cup Cornmeal
½ tsp. Salt
¼ tsp. Pepper
4 beef cube steaks (1 pound)
1 egg white
1 tsp. water
2 tbsp. oil (may need more to fry steaks)

Gravy:

1 tbsp. butter
2 tbs. all purpose flour
1½ cup milk
1 tsp. beef bouillon
½ tsp. majoram
¼ tsp. thyme
⅛ tsp. pepper

For Steak:

1. Mix 3 tbsp. flour, cornmeal, salt and pepper in a bowl; set aside. In a ziplock, put remaining flour. Put one steak at a time in bag with flour, and shake to coat.
2. In a shallow bowl, beat egg white and water, dip coated steak in egg mixture, then coat with cornmeal mixture.
3. In a skillet, heat oil. When oil is hot, cook 2 steaks, 5-7 minutes, turning once. Remove and keep warm. Cook remaining 2 steaks, adding more oil if needed. Remove keep warm.
4. Make gravy in same skillet steaks were cooked. Remove all but 1 tbsp. of steak drippings with 1 tbsp. butter. Add flour to make a rue. Slowly add milk, add remaining ingredients, and cook until thickened, stirring to prevent lumps. Remove steaks and either put in skillet with gravy and serve or serve gravy separate and pour over steaks.

SLOW COOKER MUSHROOM CHICKEN

Ingredients:

2 chicken thighs or 1 breast
1 can (10.5 oz.) cream of mushroom soup
1 can (10.5 oz.) of water
1 box Stovetop Chicken Stuffing

Directions:

1. In crockpot mix soup, water, stuffing, and mix thoroughly.
2. Add chicken.
3. Cook for 6 hours on low.

CHICKEN SATAY WITH PEANUT SAUCE

CARL HAUSHEER

When we lived in London, there was a Thai restaurant, Talad Thai, in Richmond. They had cooking classes and the best take out Thai food in town. They would marinate the chicken overnight and serve it with peanut sauce.

CHICKEN SATAY

Ingredients:

4 chicken breasts sliced and pounded with a mallet. Cut into strips.
3 cloves garlic
2 tsp. grated fresh ginger
1 tablespoon curry powder
1 teaspoon turmeric
1 teaspoon coriander
5 oz. coconut milk

Directions:

Combine powder and add a touch of oil and make into a paste. Add all ingredients and marinate chicken for a few hours in covered bowl and refrigerate.

Thread chicken onto skewers and grill on high heat 2 minutes each side. Sprinkle marinade over chicken while cooking to keep moist.

PEANUT BUTTER SAUCE

Ingredients:

8 oz. coconut milk
1 tbsp. curry powder (combine with touch of oil to make paste)
2 tbsp. smooth peanut butter
1 tbsp. sugar
1 tbsp. lemon juice
1 tbsp. fish sauce or soya sauce
Touch of salt

Directions:

Heat coconut milk over low heat, stir in paste and ingredients. Stir continuously and bring to a boil. Reduce to simmer for 5 minutes.

CHICKEN MARSALA

Ingredients:

4 skinless, boneless, chicken breasts (about 1½ pounds)
All-purpose flour, for dredging
Kosher salt and freshly ground black pepper
¼ cup extra-virgin olive oil
4 oz. prosciutto, thinly sliced
8 oz. crimini or porcini mushrooms, stemmed and halved
½ cup sweet Marsala wine
½ cup chicken stock
2 tbsp. unsalted butter
¼ cup chopped flat-leaf parsley

Directions:

Put the chicken breasts side by side on a cutting board and lay a piece of plastic wrap over them; pound with a flat meat mallet, until they are about ¼-inch thick. Put some flour in a shallow platter and season with a fair amount of salt and pepper; mix with a fork to distribute evenly.

Heat the oil over medium-high flame in a large skillet. When the oil is nice and hot, dredge both sides of the chicken cutlets in the seasoned flour, shaking off the excess. Slip the cutlets into the pan and fry for 5 minutes on each side until golden, turning once – do this in batches if the pieces don't fit comfortably in the pan. Remove the chicken to a large platter in a single layer to keep warm.

Lower the heat to medium and add the prosciutto to the drippings in the pan, sauté for 1 minute to render out some of the fat. Now, add the mushrooms and sauté until they are nicely browned and their moisture has evaporated, about 5 minutes; season with salt and pepper. Pour the Marsala in the pan and boil down for a few seconds to cook out the alcohol. Add the chicken stock and simmer for a minute to reduce the sauce slightly. Stir in the butter and return the chicken to the pan; simmer gently for 1 minute to heat the chicken through. Season with salt and pepper and garnish with chopped parsley before serving.

PULLED PORK SLIDERS

Ingredients:

1 tsp. vegetable oil
1 (4 pound) pork shoulder roast
1 cup barbecue sauce
½ cup apple cider vinegar
½ cup chicken broth
¼ cup light brown sugar
1 tbsp. prepared yellow mustard
1 tbsp. Worcestershire sauce
1 tbsp. chili powder
1 extra large onion, chopped
2 large cloves garlic, crushed
1½ tsp. dried thyme
8 hamburger buns, split
2 tbsp. butter, or as needed

Directions:

1. Pour the vegetable oil into the bottom of a slow cooker. Place the pork roast into the slow cooker; pour in the barbecue sauce,

apple cider vinegar, and chicken broth. Stir in the brown sugar, yellow mustard, Worcestershire sauce, chili powder, onion, garlic, and thyme. Cover and cook on High until the roast shreds easily with a fork, 5 to 6 hours.
2. Remove the roast from the slow cooker and shred the meat using two forks. Return the shredded pork to the slow cooker and stir the meat into the juices.
3. Spread the inside of both halves of hamburger buns with butter. Toast the buns, butter side down, in a skillet over medium heat until golden brown. Spoon pork into the toasted buns.

KIELBASA CASSEROLE

Ingredients:

4-6 servings of instant mashed potatoes
¾ cup sour cream
¾ cup shredded Swiss and sharp cheese (can use just one cheese if you prefer)
1 tbsp. minced onion (optional)
1 tbsp. parsley
½ tsp. salt
¼ cup dill weed
⅛ tsp. black pepper
1 package of kielbasa, fried up in 1" thick pieces

Directions:

1. Follow directions on box to make instant mashed potatoes. Once they're done, add in sour cream, cheese, kielbasa and all the other ingredients. Put mixture into buttered casserole dish, sprinkle a little more cheese, and a dash of paprika on top.
2. Bake at 350 degrees for 30-40 minutes. Let set for 5 minutes and enjoy!

SMOKEY CAJON HAMBURGER
CHRISTOPHER SHAW

This meat dish is a recipe that started with my first steps learning how to cook. For as long as I can remember, I spent time with myself and my siblings in our family's backyard cookouts every summer trying my hand at the grill. It was a game of trial, error, and sometimes ended in horribly burnt food, as I tried to beat out my siblings at who could make the best dish.

Ingredients:

Brioche hamburger buns
2½ lbs. ground beef
2 tsp. smoked paprika
1 tsp. salt
1 tsp. black pepper
½ tsp. dark brown sugar
¼ tsp. garlic powder
¼ tsp. onion powder
¼ tsp. ground cayenne pepper
¼ tsp. crushed red peppers
Grilled portobello mushrooms
Swiss cheese slices, tomato slices, sliced Vidalia onions

Directions:

Set buns aside to warm. Mix all ingredients together except for mushrooms and cheese. Form into 10 patties. Grill 5 minutes on each side. Slice mushrooms and grill, 3 minutes on each side. Assemble burgers in the warm brioche buns with sliced mushrooms on top.

TACO/PASTA CASSEROLE

Ingredients:

1½ pounds of ground beef or ground turkey
Taco seasoning packet
12 oz. salsa
8 oz. Mexican or taco cheese
1 lb. cooked ziti or penne pasta

Directions:

1. Cook ground beef/turkey in a pan that can be placed in the oven.
2. Follow the instructions on the taco seasoning to ground beef/turkey to cook and season the meet. Once the ground beef/turkey is cooked and seasoned, pour in one jar of salsa (or to liking) and cooked pasta. Mix all together, place the cheese on top of the mixture and place in a hot oven at 350 degrees to melt the cheese.
3. Once the cheese is fully melted, take out of the oven and serve.

QUICK GOULASH

Ingredients:

1 to 1 ½ pound of stew meat cut to ½ pieces
2 8 oz. cans of tomato sauce
2 packages of onion soup mix

Directions:

In a pan, brown the stew meat, drain the liquid out of the pan, pour the tomato sauce in the pan, with ½ can of water from each can (clean each can of remaining sauce), pour the 2-packages of onion soup mix, cook for 20 to 30 minutes, until meat is fully cooked. Serve over egg noodles, mashed potatoes, zoodles, etc.

DAD'S BLACK FOREST CHICKEN WITH BBC SAUCE

ANTIONE ADAMS

Ingredients:

3 lbs. chicken (preferably dark, but white will work as well)
1 cup canned dark soy sauce (last press: dark and thick)
¼ cup ketchup
1 tbsp. brown sugar
2 tsp. black pepper
1 tsp. salt
1 tsp. paprika
1 tsp. dried parsley
1 tsp. hot pepper sauce (Optional, for piquante)
¼ pimento (allspice) seeds (for a non-charcoal grill)

Preparation:

1. Thaw the chicken and slightly score (make shallow grooves with knife) into the meat. Leaving the skin on will allow the oil from the chicken skin to help keep the meat soft and add to the flavor, or one can remove the skin.
2. Put all the chicken into a large wide-mouth bowl and squeeze ½ lemon onto the chicken. Mix thoroughly and set aside.

3. In a large mixing bowl, put the all the sauce ingredients in and mix *well*. Pour sauce over chicken and coat thoroughly. Let stand for 1–2 hours in fridge.

Method:

1. Light grill (charcoal grill is preferable for a rich, smoky flavor).
2. Lightly coat the grill tines with oil. (Repeat this process throughout the cooking when the meat begins to stick. (Foil use *not* recommended as the meat consistency and sauce cooking will suffer.)
3. If the grill is non-charcoal, heat to about 450 degrees.
4. When hot, bring out meat. Put meat on grill.
5. Throw a large pinch of the pimento seeds directly into the fire and let the smoke curl onto the meat as you turn it. Repeat periodically throughout the entire cooking process.
6. As the sauce on the meat begins to dry on and get slightly sticky, add more sauce with a grill brush from the meat bowl. Make sure all pieces get this treatment evenly so you have to visually regulate how much sauce is brushed onto each piece
7. *The finished piece* should be well cooked, *but not dried out,* and be well coated with dark sauce with a cooked, slightly sticky texture.

For really good flavor: Cook with a beer in hand, under bright sunshine, with wife on phone and the kids running around like escaped mental patients. ENJOY.

ENCHILADA CASSEROLE

Ingredients:

1 lb. ground beef
1 medium onion
Tortillas, at least 8
1 12 oz. can diced tomatoes w/chilis
1 12 oz. can enchilada sauce
1 12 0z. can refried beans
1 12 oz. can black beans
1 packet taco seasoning

Directions:

1. Preheat oven to 350 degrees.
2. Brown meat with diced onion.
3. Add taco seasoning, drained green chilis with diced tomatoes.
4. CASSEROLE DISH: Line with tortillas, layer of meat (half of the meat), layer of grated cheddar, enchilada sauce, tortillas, meat, cheese, sauce, beans on top.
5. Bake for 30 minutes.

VEGAN SLOPPY JOE'S

Ingredients:

Olive oil, to taste
½ medium yellow onion, diced
½ green or red bell pepper, diced
2 cloves garlic, minced
1 teaspoon chili powder
1 jalapeño diced
Salt to taste
1 cup TVP (Textured Vegetable Protein)
1 cup vegetable broth
12 oz. crushed plum tomatoes
1½ tbsp. soy sauce
2 tsp. brown sugar
1 tsp. Dijon mustard
4 hamburger buns

Directions:

1. In a medium skillet, heat a drizzle of olive oil over medium heat. Once the oil begins to shimmer, add the onion and cook for 2-3 minutes until semi-translucent.
2. Add the bell pepper and cook for another 2-3 minutes until the onion is translucent.
3. Add the garlic, chili powder, and salt and cook 2-3 minutes more until the garlic is soft and fragrant. Season with salt.
4. Add the textured vegetable protein, vegetable broth, jalapeño and tomato and stir well until combined. Cover and cook for 15 minutes until most of the liquid has been absorbed.
5. Remove the lid and add the soy sauce, brown sugar, and Dijon mustard. Mix to combine and cook for 3-4 more minutes until the remaining liquid has been absorbed.
6. Serve on hamburger buns and enjoy!

FARRO RISOTTO WITH SHRIMP

Ingredients:

2 cups low sodium chicken broth
2 tbsp. extra virgin olive oil
4 scallions, white and green parts separated and thinly sliced
½ cups pearled farro
½ cup dry white wine
1 lb. medium shrimp, peeled and deveined
1 cup frozen sweet peas, thawed
¼ cup finely grated parmesan
¼ cup finely shopped fresh basil and parsley, mixed plus whole leaves for garnish
Coarse salt and freshly ground pepper

Directions:

Bring broth and 2 cups of water to a simmer in a medium saucepan. In a separate medium saucepan heat oil on medium. Add scallion whites and cook in oil, stirring frequently until translucent, about 2 minutes.

Add farro, stirring constantly, until toasted, about another 2 minutes. Add white wine and cook, stirring until absorbed.

Add ½ cup broth mixture to farro and cook, stirring constantly until absorbed. Continue adding ½ cup at a time until faro is tender, but still slightly firm. Constant stirring releases the starches and brings about a slightly milky texture. About 30 to 45 minutes. Stir in shrimp and peas and cook until shrimp are opaque. Stir in cheese, scallion greens, and chopped herbs. Season with salt and pepper.

HEART HEALTHY SHRIMP SCAMPI

Ingredients:

1-1½ lb. of shrimp, cleaned and de-veined
2 tbsp. of extra virgin olive oil (EVOO)
1 bottle of clam juice
Juice of 1 lemon
1 tsp. crushed red pepper flakes
3 cloves of garlic chopped
Fresh parsley, split in two section
Corn starch to desired thickness

Directions:

1. Put one tablespoon of EVOO in a hot pan, cook shrimp until pink, then remove.
2. Using the remaining EVOO, cook the garlic, then pour in clam juice, crushed pepper flakes, and the juice of one lemon. Cook until starting to boil, turn down to a simmer, and add corn starch one teaspoon at a time to a desired thickness.
3. Once at desired thickness, return shrimp for about one minute

and then garnish with fresh parsley and serve over pasta, zoodles, rice, etc.

PAN SEARED SCALLOPS

Ingredients:

Frozen (thawed) or fresh scallops
2 tbsp. extra virgin olive oil (EVOO)
2-3 cloves of sliced garlic or tablespoon or minced garlic
1 cup of white, rose, or zinfandel wine
Fresh parsley or another garnish

Directions:

1. In a hot pan, heat 1 tbsp. olive oil. Once hot, cook the scallops (about 2-3 minutes per side depending on the side). Once cooked, take the scallops out; use the remaining tbsp. in the hot pan. Once hot, put the garlic in the pan until cooked.
2. When the garlic is done, pour the wine into the pan and put the scallops in the pan. Let everything blend for a bit.
3. Serve over pasta, rice, zoodles, cauliflower rice, etc and garish with the fresh parsley.

TIN FOIL FISH GRILL
PAUL CUMMINGS

This is great way to cook your catch on the grill or broiler! Repeat this process for each person you plan to feed!

Ingredients:

2 filets or one cleaned pan fish
3-5 small red skinned potatoes, halved
1 fresh Jersey tomato, quartered
A few slices of red onion
1 fresh clove of garlic, diced
Old Bay seasoning
Butter or olive oil
2-3 slices of lemon
Aluminum foil, one foot square

Directions:

Take your aluminum foil and fold it to make a bowl shape. Lay your fish on the bottom and dust with Old Bay seasoning. Add your veggies around the fish, and then lay the three slices of lemon atop it all. Now either drizzle the whole pile with olive oil, liberally, or lay half a stick of unsalted butter in the mix (the heat from the grill will melt it for you). Now fold closed the top of the foil and cut a small triangle flap, so later you can check the contents on the grill.

Place the whole foil tent on a hot grill, high heat, and wait 5 minutes. After 5 minutes check the flap and assure the fish has a nice white color, or if it is a pan fish, check that the meat and skin are opaque. Close the flap and wait 2 more minutes. There should be ample steam coming from the flap when the fish is done.

Remove from heat, wait two minutes to cool the foil, and eat it out of the foil!

Easy clean-up, I will be there at 7, keep the beer cold.

SMOKED FISH AND SMOKED FISH SALAD

PAUL CUMMINGS

This is a great way to clear out your freezer, or use up a lot of fish!

Ingredients:

3-4 lbs. of fish filet, steaks, or pan fish
1 cup brown sugar
1 cup apple cider vinegar
½ cup sea Salt
Alderwood and Applewood Wood Chips

Directions:

You need to brine your fish overnight. Use a gallon of warm water in a sealable container to mix the vinegar, sugar, and salt. Immerse all your fish in the container, and seal it. Keep this cool (a refrigerator works) overnight. Drain the fish and arrange them in a smoker. Hot smoking requires roughly 6 hours. For the best flavor, alternate between Alder and Applewood wood chips. The process will cure and cook the fish. Ready to eat as it is!

BUT... if you are feeling adventurous...

Add one pound of boneless smoked fish to 1 cup of mayonnaise, a sprinkle of Old Bay seasoning, and 3 (or more) teaspoons of Franks Red Hot Sauce or Tabasco Chipolte Pepper sauce. Serve on a bun and you have one helluva great sandwich spread! I have been known to eat it from the container, and I stopped telling friends and family when I was making this...moochers.

CAPT PAUL'S FISHCAKES
PAUL CUMMINGS

This is great way to cook your catch on the oven, broiler, or frying pan!

Ingredients:

1 lb. fish filets
1 onion, diced finely
2 cups Italian style bread crumbs
1 bottle Thousand Island salad dressing
Old Bay seasoning
1 raw egg

Directions:

1. Take the boneless fish filets and microwave them for about thirty seconds, so they flake and whiten very slightly.
2. Using your hands, mix the flaked fish, onion, and bread crumbs, making sure you have an even blend of all three ingredients.
3. Next mix in your egg and salad dressing to moisten and bind the whole mix together. Knead this with your hands until you have the consistency of ground meat.

4. Now form into fish patties to the size you desire and bake at 350 degrees or fry on high heat until firm and brown but not burnt.
5. I prefer mine with cocktail sauce on a bun. This should serve 4 people.

CRAB BOIL

PAUL CUMMINGS

This is the easiest way to use up any crabs you get...

Ingredients:

One large, deep pot (3 gallons+)
Medium-size crabs, stone or blue claw (up to 10 at a time)
Lemon wedges
1 can of beer, your choice, recommend a pilsner
Old Bay seasoning

Directions:

1. Assure your crabs are alive. Dead crabs can be dangerous to eat.
2. Over a stovetop or outside boiler, bring one gallon of water to a boil. Add one can of beer, season with Old Bay, and drop in crabs. Uncooked crabs will sink, cooked crabs will float.
3. Crabs are cooked when their shells change color to a rusty orangeish-red color with tan on the joints. Carefully remove crabs from the boiling water mixture, adding more if necessary.

4. Let cooked crabs sit for 5 minutes to cool, and enjoy with lemon. As simple as it can get.

BEER BOILED FISH

PAUL CUMMINGS

This is a great way to fry your fish WITHOUT any oils or greases!

Ingredients:

1 lb. of white meat fish fillets, or steaks butterflied.
1 can of beer (I recommend a lighter beer or lager)
Old Bay seasoning

Directions:

1. In a deep frying pan, on high heat, pour ½ can of beer. Sprinkle liberally with Old Bay seasoning. Lay filets into the beer as it starts to heat.
2. Flip at first boil, continually flipping the filets as the beer boils off. Sprinkle with Old Bay seasoning before the last of the beer boils off.
3. Fish is done when the beer is done!
4. This is a tartar sauce kind of meal. What you do with that other half of beer is entirely up to you!

GINGER SCALLION SHRIMP

Ingredients:

Marinade:

½ tsp. salt
¼ tsp. sugar
1 tsp. soy sauce
¼ tsp. white pepper powder
¼ tsp. garlic powder
½ tsp. corn starch
½ lb. frozen shrimp or fresh

Directions:

1. Defrost frozen shrimp. Rinse and drain.
2. Cut off shrimp feelers and heads.
3. Marinate shrimp for 3-4 hours (save marinade).
4. Air dry shrimp in strainer or use paper towels to soak up excess water.
5. Heat wok under high heat.
6. Test wok by dripping water droplet – evaporate on contact.

7. Add 1 tablespoon vegetable oil.
8. Add 3-4 smashed garlic cloves wedges.
9. Add ginger root – cut into matchsticks.
10. Stir fry in oil.
11. Add air dried shrimp. Stir fry until shrimp begins to curl.
12. Add scallions – 1-2" strips.
13. Stir fry together
14. Add leftover marinade and 1 tablespoon of water for gravy.
15. Stir fry together.

GRILLED TILEFISH

Ingredients:

3-4 tilefish filets
1 stick butter
1 tsp. chopped parsley
1 tsp. minced garlic
2 tbsp. salt
2 tbsp. pepper

Golden tilefish live along the continental shelf in depths ranging from 400-900'. They are extremely flavorful and have been compared to lobster by many who I fish with. This recipe seems extremely simple...it is. Tiles do not require anything fancy...give it a shot and enjoy!

Directions:

1. Pat dry filets prior to cooking. Do not wash the fish in fresh water as it degrades the product
2. Place two or three tilefish filets on a piece of aluminum foil that is approx. 5" larger on all sides than the footprint of the filets.

3. Cut a stick of butter into cross-section slices that are approx. ⅛" thick. Place on top of the filets close enough so when they melt the entire filet is exposed to butter.
4. Lightly sprinkle salt, pepper, chopped parsley, and minced garlic over the filets. Depending on size of filets, a half teaspoon of salt and pepper should be enough. I usually use a teaspoon of parsley and garlic.
5. Take another piece of foil and cover the filets. Crimp the edges of the top and bottom layers of foil together to prevent melted butter from escaping.
6. Place on grill for approx. 8-10 min. or until fish are cooked through.

SPICY SEARED SEA SCALLOPS

Ingredients:

2 pounds large sea scallops, about 18 to 20
2 tsp. Cajun seasoning
2 tsp. extra virgin olive oil
½ tsp. salt
Dash freshly ground pepper
1 tbsp. extra virgin olive oil
2 tsp. unsalted butter

Directions:

1. In a bowl or food storage bag, toss scallops gently with the Cajun seasoning, 2 tsp. olive oil, salt, and pepper. Refrigerate for about 1 hour.
2. In a skillet, heat 1 tbsp. olive oil.
3. Sear each side of scallop.

HONEY GARLIC SHRIMP

Ingredients:

⅓ cup honey
¼ cup soy sauce (I use reduced sodium)
1 tbsp. jarred minced garlic or 2 tsp. fresh*
Optional: 1 teaspoon minced fresh ginger
1 lb. medium uncooked shrimp, peeled & deveined
2 tsp. olive oil
Optional: chopped green onion for garnish

Directions:

1. Whisk the honey, soy sauce, garlic, and ginger (if using) together in a medium bowl.
2. Place shrimp in a large zipped-top bag or Tupperware. Pour ½ of the marinade mixture on top, give it all a shake or stir, then allow shrimp to marinate in the refrigerator for 15 minutes or for up to 8-12 hours. Cover and refrigerate the rest of the marinade for step 3. (Time-saving tip: while the shrimp is marinating, I steam broccoli and microwave some quick brown rice.)

3. Heat olive oil in a skillet over medium-high heat. Place shrimp in the skillet. (Discard used marinade.) Cook shrimp on one side until pink – about 45 seconds – then flip shrimp over. Pour in remaining marinade and cook it all until shrimp is cooked through, about 1 minute more.
4. Serve shrimp with cooked marinade sauce and a garnish of green onion. The sauce is excellent on brown rice and steamed veggies on the side.
5. Heat the 1 tbsp. olive oil and 2 tsp. of butter in a large skillet over high heat. With tongs, arrange the scallops in the hot fat and cook for about 2 to 3 minutes on each side or until nicely browned.

YUM NEAU OR LARB NEAU OR LARB GAI YUM NEAU OR LARB NEAU OR LARB GAI

THAI BEEF OR CHICKEN SALAD
(Neau is for beef. Larb is for ground. Gai is for chicken)

Meat Options:
London broil
Tri-tip
97% lean ground beef or ground sirloin
Ground pork
Ground chicken
Boneless skinless chicken breast

Vegetables:
Scallion or also called green onion
Cilantro or also called coriander
Red onion

Other:
Limes 6-12

Fish sauce

Ground roasted rice powder

Course ground chili pepper

Fresh chili pepper

White rice usually jasmine or minute rice works (never tried brown rice with it)

Bak Choi (Chinese cabbage) use an an optional wrap usually with the ground meats

Coffee grinder

Mortar and pestle

Optional (Accent MSG): It's not necessary, it's just a meat enhancer that my mom has used in everything so I still use it. Some can't tell the difference, I taught some people how to make it and they didn't use MSG and I could tell the difference. You are just using small amounts. Your choice.

MEAT PREPARATION

LONDON BROIL

1. Broil or grill London broil or Tri-tip to medium rare. You want a nice pink to reddish in the center.
2. Slice London broil or Tri-tip into 4 quarters.
3. Then slice each quarter at an angle like you would a roast, thin slices.

GROUND MEATS

1. Prepare in skillet or frying pan just as if you were making Hamburger Helper without adding anything, just maybe a little salt and pepper.
2. Cook until browned. I usually like ground meat to be cooked a little longer but as long as it is completely cooked through.

CHICKEN BREAST

1. This one is new. Take the chicken breasts, as many or as few as you like and put them in a broiler pan (I don't have a grill) and fill the bottom with water.
2. Place the chicken above the water. (My broiler pan comes with this piece, otherwise just fill something that can be baked with water and put the chicken onto something that will fit over whatever you put the water in.)
3. Douse the chicken with lime juice, fresh or concentrate and a little garlic salt and course ground black pepper.
4. Cook until nice and golden brown.
5. Turn over and do the same
6. The water keeps the chicken moist while the outside roasts and gets a crust like texture.
7. After both sides are cooked, slice at an angle much like the London broil. Thin slices.

<u>VEGETABLE PREPARATION</u>

<u>SCALLION</u>

1. Slice green onion into thin slices (little circles).
2. Use as much of the white part as possible since this is where the strongest flavor comes from.

<u>CILANTRO</u>

1. Grab a bushel and twist just beneath the main canopy of leaves and remove the stems in a twisting motion. It is ok to have some of the stems, you just don't want it to be all stems.
2. Chop to desired fineness. Usually just a once over with a good knife and you're done.

<u>RED ONION</u>

1. Chop into quarters and then cut thin slices from each quarter.

MEATLOAF

Ingredients:

1 lb. lean ground beef
1 lb. ground turkey
2 eggs
½ cup tomato sauce or organic ketchup
1 cup bread crumbs
1 tsp. garlic
1 tsp. salt
1 tsp. pepper
1 tsp. oregano

Directions:

1. Mix well to combine all ingredients.
2. Form into loaf or use a loaf pan. (I put mine onto a baking sheet, formed into a loaf.)
3. Bake at 350 degrees for 1 hour.

CHICKEN GOLDEN CURRY RECIPE

Ingredients:

Beef (or chicken, lamb, shrimp), chopped
Medium onion, sliced
Medium carrot, chopped
Celery, chopped
Potatoes, chopped/diced no skin
Vegetable oil
Water
Thai Coconut can (1)
S&B Golden Curry Sauce Mix - 1 Pack

Directions:

1. Stir-fry the onions and vegetables with vegetable oil in a large skillet on medium heat for approx. 5 min. or till golden brown.
2. Add the choice of meat, my personal fav. is chicken. Add salt and fresh ground pepper.
3. Add water and Thai Coconut (1 can) to top level and bring to boil. Reduce heat, cover and simmer until ingredients are tender, approx. 15-20 mins.

4. Turn the heat off, break S&B Golden Curry Sauce Mix into pieces and add them to the skillet. Stir until sauce mixes are completely melted. Simmer approx. 5 min., stirring constantly. The consistency must be like oatmeal.
5. Serve hot over white rice.

Favorite Dish: First dish that I learned how to cook when I lived with a roommate after college during my professional career.

COCONUT CURRY IN A HURRY RECIPE

Ingredients:

2 tbsp. coconut oil
1 medium yellow onion, diced
1 lb. chicken, beef, or pork cut into bite-sized pieces
3 cloves minced garlic
1 tbsp. chopped fresh ginger
2 tsp. ground coriander
1 or 2 tsp. red pepper flakes for spice (optional)
1 can (13 oz.) coconut milk
1 cup shredded carrots
2 or 3 tbsp. yellow curry paste
1 tsp. salt
½ teaspoon freshly ground black pepper
4 medium red or Yukon gold potatoes, cut into bite-sized pieces
3 cups fresh spinach leaves (optional)
1 tbsp. lime juice
2 tbsp. brown sugar

Directions:

1. Place cut potatoes on a baking sheet and bake in an oven preheated to 350 degrees for 20 minutes, then set aside.
2. Add oil to skillet and sauté onions until they soften and just begin to turn brown.
3. Season chicken, pork, or beef with salt & pepper, then add to the skillet. Sauté until chicken, pork, or beef is fully cooked.
4. Add garlic, ginger, coriander to the skillet. Cook until fragrant (about 1 minute).
5. Stir in coconut milk, yellow curry paste, and carrots. Add salt & pepper to taste.
6. Simmer over medium heat for about 5 minutes and allow liquid to reduce to desired thickness.
7. Stir in brown sugar, lime juice, red pepper flakes, potatoes, and spinach. Cook for about 2 mins.
8. Taste and adjust seasoning as desired.
9. Serve over rice and garnish with chopped basil or cilantro.

GOULASH

Ingredients:

1½ lb. stew beef- cut into 1 inch cubes
1 lg. onion, sliced
1+ scoop flour
1 tsp. caraway seeds
3-4 bay leaves
Vegetable oil
Salt & pepper

Directions:

1. In large pot, brown stew beef in oil. Add and brown onion slices in same pan. Stir in a scoop of flour until meat and onion are well coated. Cover with water and stir well.
2. Add salt, pepper, caraway seeds, and bay leaves. Cover and let simmer until beef is tender, being careful not to let it boil. Add additional water if needed.
3. Thicken gravy before serving with cornstarch & water or flour & water.

4. Serve over rye or pumpernickel bread, noodles, potato dumplings, or mashed potatoes.

GUMBO

Roux:
1 stick butter
2 tbsp. olive oil
1 cup flour

Directions:

Heat in skillet and stir consistently until the roux is color of a copper penny

Ingredients:

4 large chicken breasts
2 lb. of sausage
2 onions
1 bell pepper

Directions:

1. Boil 1 gallon of water with 4 large chicken breasts until chicken is cooked.
2. Remove chicken and de-bone/shred chicken.

3. Add roux to boiling water, stirring until roux dissolves entirely.
4. Add chopped onions and bell pepper.
5. Add shredded chicken.
6. Cut sausage in to small chunks and add to gumbo.
7. Add pepper, salt, garlic, Tony Chatcherie's seasoning to taste.
8. Add Gumbo file to taste.

Hard boil a dozen eggs, peel, and put in the gumbo.

BRISKET

Ingredients:

4 or 5 pound brisket
1-2 packages of Lipton's Onion Soup Mix
Garlic powder
3-4 potatoes cut into chunks
3-4 carrots cut into chunks

Directions:

1. Wash brisket and place into a roasting pan.
2. Sprinkle with 1 or 2 packets of the onion soup mix all over the raw brisket and sprinkle with garlic powder also.
3. Pour 2 cups of water around the sides of the meat. Place the potatoes and carrots around the meat.
4. Bake in a 350 degree oven for approximately 3-4 hours or until soft.

GRILLED CHEESE SANDWICH WITH PICKLES

BILL BARSTCH

You go out and work in the cold. On the water if possible.

Come home to empty house or everyone else asleep in middle of the night.

Take out whatever bread they left you. Heals from a loaf that's been used as a natural "stay fresh" bread lid for a week works well enough.

Break out good sharp cheddar. Place too much on a slice of bread.

Put three quality Bread and Butter pickle slices on a plate and microwave for 15 seconds.

Put warmed pickles on cheese.

Put a little too much butter in the pan.

Put second slice of bread atop the first one with the stuff on it.

Cook sandwich in pan until in smells like potential trouble. Then flip the sandwich and repeat on other side.

Let some cheese slide out of the sandwich as you go and make sure it gets fused onto the exterior of the sandwich here and there.

Take sandwich and a beer outside if possible to eat. If too cold out, sit by a window.

Eat in full view of your dog or cat. Tell them how you deserve it and that you pay for everything they need.

After done, let animal lick the butter off your fingers and contemplate opening a second beer.

Nap afterwards.

PART SEVEN
DESSERT

Back in 2004, I was stationed on the Soderman. I caught the ship in Japan, and we were heading east across the Pacific to Seattle and then down to LA Long Beach. While the destination is important, it is not the focus of the story. Along with the regular crew that I have sailed with on multiple voyages, there were a few new faces among the crew. One of these was a cadet from a very reputable maritime institution (I will not say which one), and he was very proud of the school he attended (not surprising) and the state from which he hailed (surprising). Not only was he from the smallest state in the U.S,, he had the body frame and the Napoleonic complex to match. We'll call him Ed (Special Ed behind his back).

So, we depart the coast of Japan and begin our trek east. I should also point out that Ed was well versed in everything about everything (according to him, anyway). He was very quick to voice his opinion, express his point of view, or attempt to correct our thought process, regardless of its accuracy. To put it mildly, he had a classic case of "Bullshit-itis!" As you can imagine, this practice was more than a little tiring. Unfortunately, I had the bad luck of being on the same bridge watch with him (midnight-4 a.m.). This made for a very long shift.

Now the timing of this next part and the positioning of where it happened is crucial to this story.

Anyone who has spent any time on the ship has endured at least a little playful hazing (Ex: Get me a bucket of steam, Go grease the Relative bearing... etc). Well, we were approaching the international date line during our shift and I approached the mate on watch. It was one of those conversations that goes, "Wouldn't it be funny if...?" Little did I realize that his sense of humor rivaled my own, and he agreed to go with my "what if" scenario.

The call came across the radio for the cadet to report to the mate on watch on the bridge...and then we waited. As soon as Ed showed up, the mate on watch followed my lead. I informed Ed that it was "imperative" that we record the exact second that we crossed the International Date Line. (I'm sure that part is true... Here's the part that's not). I also informed him that to mark the International Date Line, the Coast Guard set up a series of mirrored buoys that formed an iridescent green line in the water marking precisely where the date line was. His response was priceless... "Oh, I've heard of that before!" (He hadn't because it doesn't exist, but there wasn't a snowball's chance in hell that we were going to tell him that.)

The bait was cast and he took the hook. We gave Ed a radio, a blacklight flashlight (to see the line better, of course) and asked him to check in every fifteen minutes from the bow. So, while we were up on the bridge sipping coffee, Ed was giving us quarterly reports from the bow that he still had not seen the line yet. We crossed the International Date Line around 2 am, and we called Ed in from the bow at 3:45 and asked for a detailed report. He said that he was on continuous watch but never did see the buoys and could never see the green line.

The mate on watch feigned irritation, and with a straight face advised that Ed needed to report to the captain in the morning and request an ID-10-T form (for those that ever served as a Marine, ID-10-T spelled out is Idiot). The next morning, the mate on watch and I sat and watched the show as Ed marched up to Captain Mike and requested an ID-10-T form for not reporting the "Green Line" in the water marking the International Date Line the previous night on watch.

Captain Mike, knowing our devious sense of humor, looked in our direction and raised a single eyebrow. He leaned into the cadet's ear, pulled him in close and said, "Son, you've been had! Id-10-T stands for idiot! Might I advise that, moving forward, a little humility and a little less buffoonery might be warranted!"

There's nothing like having a whole "Humble Pie" thrown in your face to bring you back to reality. Ed was pissed, but he was also smart enough to take the hint.

After that little experience, Ed learned a skill not taught in school... Humility!

Keith Gibney

CHOCOLATE ROLL

Ingredients:

6 eggs - separated
¾ cup sugar
6 tbsp. cocoa
1½ tsp. vanilla
¾ tsp. salt
1½ tsp. baking powder
Heavy cream for whipping. (1 pint is not enough and 1 quart is too much, but it is better to have extra whipped cream.)

Directions:

1. Preheat oven to 350 degrees.
2. Cream together egg yolks and sugar. Add cocoa, salt, baking powder and vanilla. Mix with a spoon.
3. Beat egg whites in a separate large bowl until very bubbly. You do not want them to be as firm as meringue, but almost. Fold the egg whites into the cocoa mixture
4. Have parchment paper on the pan and pour in batter. Bake at

350 degrees for 20 mins. or a little more. Cake is done when a toothpick poked into the middle of the cake comes out clean.
5. Loosen the sides and turn pan upside-down over a dish towel. Scrape the parchment paper off the cake. If you have used a jelly-roll pan, roll the cake in the towel while it is still hot. This way, the cake will cool in a rolled position and may not crack when you roll it later. If you have used a lasagna pan, just let the cake cool flat on the towel.
6. After the cake has cooled, whip the heavy cream until it peaks and add some sugar until it is to your liking. If you are going to have a roll, gently unroll the cake and spread with whipped cream. Place on a platter and cover the roll with whipped cream. If you have a flat cake, cut it into thirds. Place bottom layer on a platter, cover with whipped cream, add next layer, and so on.

GRILLED PEACHES

Ingredients:

2 ripe peaches, halved and pitted
¼ cup maple syrup or honey
1 tsp. cinnamon sugar
4 scoops vanilla ice cream
4 tbsp. strawberry preserves

Directions:

1. Place the peach halves into a sandwich-sized plastic zipper bag with the syrup/honey and cinnamon sugar. Let marinate in the refrigerator for at least 30 minutes.
2. Light a grill and clean the grill surface it with a wire brush.
3. Place the peaches on the grill, 2-3 minutes on each side. Save the leftover syrup marinated in the zipper bag.
4. Place each peach half pit-side up in a bowl. Place 1 tbsp. strawberry preserves on each peach where the pit was.
5. Top each peach with a scoop of vanilla ice cream and drizzle the remaining syrup marinate on top.

QUICK DESSERT

Chocolate or Vanilla

Ingredients:

1 Pkg. Oreo Cookies or Nilla Wafers
2 Tubs of Cool Whip
2 Boxes Chocolate Pudding or Vanilla Pudding
Mix up pudding according to box.

Directions:

1. In a 13x9 baking pan or foil pan, put a layer of lightly crushed Oreos or whole Nilla Wafers on bottom.
2. Add a layer of pudding.
3. Add a layer of Cool Whip.
4. Then another layer of cookies.
5. Repeat steps 2-4.
6. If doing the vanilla version, you can crush Nilla Wafers for the final top layer.

TUGBOAT RICE PUDDING

(This produces a pudding with softer consistency than traditional rice pudding)

Ingredients:

2 quarts whole milk
1 cup long grain Rice (must be long grain)
1 cup of sugar
2 tbsp. unsalted butter
1 tsp. of vanilla
2 large eggs
1 cup of heavy cream
Cinnamon to taste
Pinch of salt

Directions:

1. In a heavy saucepan cook milk, rice, sugar, butter, vanilla and pinch of salt over moderately low heat stirring every 3 minutes until rice is tender, about 1 hour.

2. Just before rice mixture is finished cooking, in a bowl beat eggs.
3. Remove rice pan from heat and immediately whisk one cup of rice mixture slowly into eggs. Stir egg mixture back into rice mixture and then stir in the cream.
4. Pour rice pudding into serving dish and sprinkle with cinnamon.
5. Chill pudding at least 3 hours. Covered pudding keeps well for 3 days.
6. Serve pudding with whip cream.

APPLE AND PEAR CAKE WITH PINE NUTS

Ingredients:

4 eggs
¾ cups sugar
1 cup flour
1 tsp. vanilla sugar
2 tsp. baking powder
3 apples
3 pears
4 tbsp. lemon juice
30-50 g butter
1 dl pine nuts

Directions:

1. Beat egg and sugar together.
2. Combine all the dry ingredients with the wet.
3. Cut the peeled apples and pears into wedges and mix with the lemon juice. Combine the fruit carefully with the batter. Pour into a buttered springform pan.

4. Sprinkle pine nuts on top of the cake and put small pieces of butter evenly over the top of the cake. Bake in oven for 45 minutes at 175°C (350°F).
5. After cake has cooled down, sprinkle powdered sugar over it.
6. Serve with ice cream.

FRENCH CHOCOLATE CAKE

Ingredients:

250g (9 oz.) bittersweet chocolate
250g (9 oz.) unsalted butter
2 ½ dl (1 cup) sugar
1¾ dl (¾ cup) all-purpose flour
1 tsp. vanilla sugar (or 2 teaspoons vanilla essence)
2 tbsp. Cointreau or Triple sec
Grated zest of 1 orange
4 eggs, separated
Chocolate glaze
125g (4½ oz.) bittersweet chocolate
1 dl (scant ½ cup) whipping cream
Pecans for decoration

Directions:

1. Preheat the oven to 180°C (350°F).
2. Grease 24 cm (9") springform pan.
3. Melt the chocolate with the butter. Add the sugar, flour, vanilla, Cointreau, orange zest, and egg yolks, mixing well.

Beat the egg whites into stiff peaks, then fold in the chocolate mixture. Pour into the prepared pan and bake 30 minutes. The cake should be completely cool before glazing.

4. Melt the chocolate with the cream. Remove from the heat and let cool for about 5 minutes. Whisk the mixture lightly, then spread over cake.
5. Garnish with pecans.

JACOBINE KAKE FROM 1919

ERIK LARSEN

This was a recipe from Erik W. Larsen '99 great grandmother who was married to Capt. Leonard Larsen who started his career on sailing vessels in Norway and sailed during the transition to steam.

Ingredients:

1 cup raisins
2 cups flour
1 cup sugar
1 cup water
6 tbsp. butter
1 tsp. cinnamon
1 tsp. ground nutmeg
1 teaspoon ground clove
½ tsp. baking powder
1 tsp. baking soda
1 egg

Directions:

1. Bring raisins, sugar, butter, nutmeg, cinnamon, and clove to a boil for three minutes. Put aside to cool.
2. Mix flour, baking powder, and baking soda with wet raisin mixture. And add the egg last.
3. Bake in oven for 45-60 minutes at 180°C (360°F).

TILSLØRTE BONDEPIKER
"VEILED FARM GIRLS"

Ingredients:

2 tbsp. unsalted butter
1½ cups breadcrumbs
3 tbsp. sugar
1 tsp. cinnamon
2 cups heavy (whipping) cream
1½ cups applesauce, *see recipe below*

Apple Sauce:
8-10 apples Golden Delicious or Fiji apples, peeled, cored and cut into cubes
½ cup sugar
½ cup water
1 Cinnamon stick (optional)
1 Vanilla stick (optional)

Directions:

1. Peel and core apples. Cut the apples into pieces and place them in a pot. Add water and sugar and add the optional

ingredients if you choose to do so. Bring to a boil and cook, stirring until the apples are soft. Let cool to room temperature.
2. In a pan, add breadcrumbs, sugar, cinnamon and butter. Stir constantly over medium heat until breadcrumbs are uniformly toasted and golden. Remove from heat and let cold.
3. In a large bowl, whip cream until stiff.
4. Layer applesauce, bread crumbs and cream in one glass bowl or individual bowls. It's best to have at least two layers.

You can easily make your own nontraditional variations by altering the applesauce by adding raisins or cranberries. One can substitute pears for apples if preferred.

SNICKERDOODLE

This recipe is a well-loved favorite, enjoyed by many crews on various ships over the past 33 years. My mother-in-law was the first person to send these to me, back when I was a Third Mate on the Overseas Arctic. Now my wife sends batches of these to the crew around the holidays. Its a dairy-free recipe, so it travels well. Enjoy.

Ingredients:

1 cup shortening (Crisco butter flavor is best)
1½ cup sugar
2 eggs
2½ cup all purpose flour
2 tsp. creme of tartar
1 tsp. baking soda
½ tsp. salt
½ cup sugar
1 tbsp cinnamon

Directions:

1. Combine flour, creme of tartar, baking soda, and salt in a bowl. Set aside.
2. Mix sugar and shortening with a hand or stand mixer. Add eggs and beat until fluffy. Add flour mixture, 1 cup at a time and mix well.
3. Chill dough for 2 hours.

To prepare cookies:

1. Preheat oven to 375 degrees.
2. Line cookie sheet with parchment paper.
3. Combine ½ cup sugar and cinnamon in a small bowl. Set aside.
4. Roll dough into 1 inch balls (about the size of a cherry tomato) then roll in sugar/cinnamon mixture and place 4 inches apart on cookie sheet.
5. Bake 8-10 minutes until edges are very slightly brown. Remove from oven and transfer to cooling rack.

ZUCCHINI BREAD

Ingredients:

3 cups all-purpose flour
1 tsp. salt
1 tsp. baking soda
1 tsp. baking powder
1 tbsp. ground cinnamon
3 eggs
1 cup vegetable oil
2¼ cup sugar
3 tsp. vanilla
2 cups grated zucchini
1 cup chopped walnuts (optional)

Directions:

1. Grease and flour two 8 x 4 loaf pans. Preheat oven to 325 degrees.
2. Sift flour, salt, baking soda, baking powder and cinnamon in a bowl.

3. In a separate larger bowl beat eggs, oil, sugar and vanilla. Add two-thirds of sifted ingredients and mix well. Add zucchini, mix. Add remaining sifted ingredients, mix.
4. Pour batter into pans.
5. Bake 50-70 minutes until tester comes out clean.
6. Cool in pan for 10 minutes, remove from pan, and let cool completely.

I make this zucchini bread every year around the holidays and give them out to neighbors, friends, and co-workers. It's become a tradition, and everyone I know who has received one waits for it each year. The list of recipients is getting bigger, a total of 60 loafs in 2019.

Captain Lindsay M. Price

GREEK MILK PIE

Ingredients:

2 lb. sugar
8 oz. sugar
14 oz. water
1 tbsp. honey
7 oz. heavy cream
3.5 oz. semolina
¼ tsp. vanilla
4 eggs
2 oz. butter, softened
1 pkg. phyllo sheets
1 cup melted butter

Directions:

1. Preheat oven to 345 degrees.
2. Mix together 2 lbs. sugar, water, and honey. Boil for 3 minutes and then let it cool down. This is your syrup.

3. In a separate bowl, mix together cream, semolina, and vanilla. Stir for 1 minute.
4. Whisk 4 eggs in another bowl, slowly ladle in cream mixture and stir. Add about 3 to 4 ladles and mix thoroughly. Add egg mixture back into original cream mixture and whisk. Add butter and 8 oz. sugar until mixture thickens.
5. On baking sheet, spread a layer of melted butter. Add first sheet of phyllo, spread butter on top of first sheet, place a second sheet of phyllo. Ladle a generous portion of custard mix in the center. Fold right side on top, left side on top of that. From bottom up, fold until you have a rectangular shaped pocket pie.
6. Repeat the process until custard is finished.
7. On top of each milk pie, spread melted butter.
8. Bake at 345 degrees for 30 minutes.
9. Drizzle with your syrup and cinnamon.

PURPLE PLUM TORTE

Ingredients:

½ cup butter, softened
1 cup sugar
2 large eggs
1 cup flour
1 tsp. baking powder
12 small purple plums, pitted and halved
1 tbsp. sugar
2 tsp. lemon juice
2 tsp. ground cinnamon

Directions:

1. Beat butter until fluffy. Gradually add sugar, beating well. Add eggs (one at a time), beating after each addition.
2. Combine flour and baking powder, then add it to the creamed mixture, beating well.
3. Spread the batter in the bottom of a greased 9 inch spring form pan.
4. Place plums (cut side down) on top of batter.

5. Combine 1 tsp. sugar and cinnamon, sprinkle over the plums. Drizzle lemon juice over the plums. Bake (uncovered) at 350 degrees for one hour, or until a wooden pick inserted in the center comes out clean.
6. Carefully remove the side of the springform pan. Serve warm.

IMPOSSIBLE PIE

Ingredients:

½ cup Bisquick
½ cup sugar
4 eggs
2 cups half and half
3½ oz. dried coconut flakes
1tsp vanilla extract
3 tbsp. butter

Directions:

1. Butter a 9 inch pie plate and set aside.
2. Preheat oven to 400 degrees.
3. Place all ingredients into a blender and mix until well combined.
4. Pour the batter into the buttered pies plate and bake until the custard is set, about 30-40 minutes.
5. Serve cold with a dollop of Cool Whip.

MARITIME M.U.G. CUPCAKE
DANIEL KIERNAN

This recipe is a dessert. It is a single-serve cupcake in a coffee mug.

Just the name of this recipe invokes so many memories from mug year. Specifically, the memory that sticks out the most is departure day for mug cruise. It was bittersweet saying goodbye to family for the first time, but the friends made and unique experiences made all of the lows of mug year worth it.

Ingredients:

¼ cup flower
2 tbsp. of sugar
2 tablespoons of cocoa powder
¼ tsp. of baking powder
2 tbsp. of melted butter
¼ cup of milk

Directions:

1. Mix ingredients into a microwave safe coffee mug and then microwave for 1-1½ minutes.
2. Allow to cool and then serve.

THE CENTENO FAMILY'S "NEW YORICAN CHEESECAKE FLAN"

DANIELLE CENTENO

I call this recipe the cheat flan, because achieving the perfect smooth, creamy texture in a traditional flan takes much more patience and practice to get right. I will keep perfecting my recipe the traditional way, but beside me, my whole family prefers this version of flan because it's virtually foolproof. The addition of cream cheese is basically cutting corners, but it comes out good, I have to admit, and what New Yorker doesn't love cheese cake?

There is always a mixture of laughing and yelling at each other from our family's kitchen. On this occasion, mom dropped a very large eggshell into the blender, and later chaos ensued when we couldn't find that one plate big enough to put the flan on. Typical of our loud and crazy Maritime family, full of sweetness and love, like this dish. Hope you enjoy.

Ingredients:

6 Eggs
1 8-oz. packet of cream cheese
1 can of evaporated milk (12 oz.)
1 can of sweetened condensed milk (14 oz.)
1 tsp. of vanilla extract
1 cup of white sugar
⅓ cup of whole or 2% milk

Directions:

1. Preheat oven to 350 degrees F (175 degrees C).
2. Place sweetened condensed milk, evaporated milk, eggs, cream cheese, milk, and vanilla extract in a blender; blend until smooth.
3. Place sugar in an even layer in a saucepan over medium heat. Cook until edges are brown, stirring from time to time with a spatula until caramel is an even golden brown and translucent, about 4 to 5 minutes.
4. Pour caramel into a 9-inch flan mold or baking pan; swirl so that caramel covers the entire bottom pan, do not pour on the sides. Using a strainer, pour the condensed milk mixture on top of the hardened caramel.
5. Fill a large oven-safe pot with room temperature water about 1 inch, carefully place the flan in the water bath.
6. Bake flan in the preheated oven uncovered until a damp table knife inserted into the center comes out clean, 50 minutes. Remove from oven and let stand for 5 minutes.
7. Chill flan in the refrigerator about 2 to 3 hours. Invert onto a serving plate so that caramel is on top.
8. Voila! Enjoy delicious flan with family and root for Maritime Football and Rugby!

CHOCOLATE CAKE
AMIE CARTER

Ingredients:

Vegetable oil spray for misting the pan
Flour for dusting the pan
1 package (18.25 oz.) plain devil's food or dark chocolate fudge cake mix
1 package (3.9 oz) chocolate instant pudding mix
4 large eggs
1 cup sour cream
½ cup warm water
½ cup vegetable oil, such as canola, corn, safflower, soybean, or sunflower
1½ cup semisweet chocolate chips

Directions:

1. Place a rack in the center of the oven and preheat the oven to 350 degrees. Lightly mist a 12-cup Bundt pan with vegetable oil spray, then dust with flour. Shake out the excess flour. Set the pan aside.

2. Place the cake mix, pudding mix, eggs, sour cream, warm water, and oil in a large mixing bowl. Blend with an electric mixer on low speed for 1 minute. Stop the machine and scrape down the sides of the bowl with a rubber spatula. Increase the mixer speed to medium and beat 2 to 3 minutes more, scraping the sides down again if needed. The batter should look thick and well-combined. Fold in the chocolate chips, making sure they are well distributed throughout the batter. Pour the batter into the prepared pan, smoothing it out with the rubber spatula. Place the pan in the oven.
3. Bake the cake until it springs back when lightly pressed with your finger and just starts to pull away from the sides of the pan, 45 to 50 minutes. Remove the pan from the oven and place it on a wire rack to cool for 20 minutes.
4. Run a long, sharp knife around the edge of the cake and invert it onto the rack to cool completely, 20 minutes more. Or invert it onto a serving platter to slice and serve while still warm.
5. If you choose to, you can melt some chocolate frosting in the microwave and pour it over the cake and let it cool and firm up. Makes for a really nice presentation with very little effort. Don't heat it up too much, just warmed a little so you can pour it out.

Note: Store this cake covered in aluminum foil or plastic wrap at room temperature for up to 1 week. Or freeze it, wrapped in foil, for up to 6 months. Thaw the cake overnight on the counter before serving.

PEANUT BUTTER-CHOCOLATE NO-BAKE COOKIES

Ingredients:

2 cups sugar
½ cup milk
1 stick (8 tbsp.) unsalted butter
¼ cup unsweetened cocoa powder
3 cups old-fashioned rolled oats
1 cup smooth peanut butter
1 tbsp. pure vanilla extract
Large pinch kosher salt

Directions:

1. Line a baking sheet with wax paper or parchment.
2. Bring the sugar, milk, butter, and cocoa to a boil in a medium saucepan over medium heat, stirring occasionally, then let boil for 1 minute. Remove from the heat. Add the oats, peanut butter, vanilla, and salt and stir to combine.
3. Drop teaspoonfuls of the mixture onto the prepared baking sheet and let sit at room temperature until cooled and

hardened, about 30 minutes. Refrigerate in an airtight container for up to 3 days.

CHOCOLATE PEPPERMINT BROWNIES

Ingredients:

2 sticks unsalted butter cut in to small pieces
1 lb. bittersweet chocolate, chopped
2 tsp. pure peppermint extract
4 large eggs
1¾ cup packed light brown sugar
¾ cup all purpose flour
1 tsp. fine sea salt
4 candy canes crushed

Directions:

1. Preheat oven to 350 degrees.
2. Butter 9x13 baking pan and line with parchment paper.
3. In a double boiler, combine ⅔ of the chocolate with 2 sticks of butter and stir until melted. Scrape chocolate into another bowl and let cool slightly. Add remainder chocolate and peppermint to boiler and melt.
4. In a medium bowl, whisk eggs with sugar until combined. Whisk into chocolate butter mixture until glossy and thick.

Sprinkle flower and salt until incorporated. Spread brownie batter in to baking pan and add peppermint mixture on top, then stir.
5. Bake brownies in the oven for 15 minutes. Remove and add candy canes. Bake for another 10-15 minutes until edges are set. Let cool for 2 hours in the pan.

BANANA PUDDING RECIPE

Ingredients:

1 - 14 oz. can sweetened condensed milk
1½ cups ice cold water
1 - 3.4 oz. box vanilla instant pudding mix
1 qt. heavy whipping cream
4 to 6 barely ripe bananas
2 - 12 oz. boxes Nilla Wafers
1 - 7.7 oz. jar of Nutella (optional)

Directions:

1. In a bowl, mix water, condensed milk, and pudding very well. Cover and let it sit overnight in the refrigerator. You can let it sit for 4 hours, but I prefer overnight to allow the mixture to set.
2. In another bowl, whip the heavy cream until peaks form. Then fold in the set pudding mixture until there are no yellow streaks remaining.
3. In a trifle bowl or medium size aluminum pan, you can start assembling the dessert.

4. Place ⅓ wafers at the bottom of your pan or bowl making sure the entire bottom is covered. Followed by the banana slices (1-2 bananas for each layer depending on your taste). You can also drizzle Nutella on the bananas (optional), followed by ⅓ of the pudding mixture. Make sure the mixture covers all the bananas.
5. You will do this step two more times with the wafers garnishing the top layer. You can also crush wafers and sprinkle the crumbs on top.
6. Cover the dessert and chill in the refrigerator for 4-8 hours. I think the longer the better because it'll give the wafers a chance to really soak in the pudding.

HOT CURRIED FRUIT

Ingredients:

1 large can of peach halves
1 medium can of pears
1 medium can of pineapple chunks
1 small jar of cherries
½ cup almonds - blanched
¼ cup butter - melted
¾ cup of brown sugar
1 tbsp. of curry powder

Directions:

1. Drain fruit and cut into bite-size pieces. Spread all but cherries in a shallow baking dish.
2. Arrange cherries on top of fruit. Sprinkle almonds all over. Combine sugar, melted butter, and curry powder and pour over fruit.
3. Bake at 325 degrees for 1½ hours. Serves 6.

SOUR CREAM PECAN PIE

Ingredients:

3 eggs
½ cup sour cream
½ cup dark corn syrup
1 tsp vanilla
⅛ tsp. salt
2 tbs butter, melted
1¼ cup pecans
1 cup sugar
1 unbaked (9") pie crust

Directions:

1. In medium mixing bowl, beat eggs well.
2. Stir in sour cream.
3. Add corn syrup, vanilla, sugar, salt, and butter, mixing well.
4. Stir in pecans.
5. Pour in pie shell and bake at 400 degrees for 40-45 minutes and then allow to cool for 2 hours. Pie will be slightly puffy.

GRAPE PIE

Ingredients:

8-9" pie crust-bottom and top
4 cups Concord grapes
¾ cups sugar
1½ tbsp. lemon juice
1 tbsp. quick-cooking tapioca

Directions:

1. Slip the pulp out of the grapes. Reserve the skins. Cook the pulp until the seeds loosen. Press through a colander or a Foley Food Mill to remove the seeds.
2. Combine the pulp, skins, sugar, lemon juice, and tapioca. Let mixed ingredients stand for 15 minutes.
3. Preheat oven to 450 degrees. Put bottom crust in pie pan and pour the mixture in evenly. Cover with top crust, pinch and trim the edge.
4. Sprinkle sugar on top crust and cut 6-8 slits. Bake the pie for 10 minutes at 450 degrees, then lower the heat to 350 degrees and bake for about 20 minutes more. ENJOY!

RUM CAKE

Cake Ingredients:

1 cup chopped pecans or walnuts
1 18½ oz. pkg. yellow cake mix
1¾ oz. pkg. instant vanilla pudding
4 eggs
½ cup cold water
½ cup oil (I use corn oil)
½ cup dark rum (light rum is also fine)

Glaze Ingredients:

¼ lb. butter or margarine
½ cup water
1 cup granulated sugar
½ cup rum

Cake Directions:

1. Preheat oven to 325 degrees. Grease and flour 10" tin or 12 cup Bundt pan. Sprinkle nuts over bottom of the pan. Mix all cake ingredients together. Pour batter over the nuts.
2. Bake 1 hour. Cool. Invert on serving plate. Prick top. Drizzle and smooth glaze evenly over the top and sides. Allow the cake to absorb glaze. Repeat till glaze is used up.

Glaze Directions:

1. Melt butter in saucepan. Stir in water and sugar. Boil 5 minutes, stirring constantly. Remove from heat. Stir in rum.
2. Nice served with whipped cream. Enjoy!!

BUTTERSCOTCH BROWNIES

Ingredients:

2 cups of unsifted flower
2 tsp. baking powder
1½ tsp. salt
1 pkg. butterscotch morsels
½ cup butter (stick)
1½ cups brown sugar
4 eggs
1 tsp. vanilla
1 cup of chopped nuts (optional)

Directions:

1. In large bowl melt morsels and butter over hot (not boiling) water.
2. In another bowl, mix flour, baking powder, and salt. Set aside.
3. Stir in brown sugar and melted morsels and cool 5 minutes. Beat in eggs and vanilla. Add flour mixture and nuts. Spread evenly in 15x10 pan and bake 30 minutes at 350 degrees.

The butterscotch recipe was from Joy Kisling. Her husband, Captain Rick Kisling, had a career as a pilot with TWA. He was chosen to fly Pope John Paul II back to Rome during his visit to the United States in 1999. Most memorable experience in his career. Pictured here is Captain Kisling with Pope John Paul II, without brownies.

PART EIGHT
SNACKS

SHORTBREAD COOKIES

Ingredients:

2 sticks of butter (one cup)
2 cup of flour
½ cup of sugar

Directions:

1. Knead into a ball, roll out to ½ inch thickness.
2. Cut out circles using a small glass or jar.
3. Place on parchment paper covered sheet pan.
4. Re-knead leftover cuttings, roll out and cut again.
5. Bake at 350 degrees for 15 minutes or until bottoms start to look slightly cooked.

6. Cool, place in tin or other container, will keep for a couple of months.

SOUTH OF THE BORDER MIX

Ingredients:

6 tbsp. butter
1 package taco seasoning mix, dry
1 tbsp. Worcestershire sauce
1 tsp. hot pepper sauce
8 cups Crispy Corn or Crispy Rice cereal squares or a combination
1 cup peanuts
1 cup pretzels
1 cup bite-size cheese crackers
2 tbsp. American Cheese food powder

Directions:

1. In a large microwave safe bowl, melt better on high. Stir in taco seasoning, Worcestershire sauce, and pepper sauce. Gradually add cereal, peanuts, and cheese crackers. Stir to coat evenly. Microwave on high 6 minutes, thoroughly stirring every to minutes.
2. Spread on waxed paper to cool, about 15 minutes.
3. Sprinkle American Cheese Food Powder over warm mix.

If using an oven, follow above directions, but instead of microwaving, bake at 250 degrees for 1 hour and stir every 15 minutes.

ASIAN FLAVORED SNACK MIX

Ingredients:

5 cups corn or rice cereal squares
1 cup chow mein noodles
3 tbsp. butter
1 tbsp peanut butter
½ tsp. garlic powder
½ tsp. dry mustard
½ tsp. ground ginger
2 tbsp. soy sauce
2 tbsp. packed brown sugar
1 to 2 tbsp. sliced almonds, optional
1 to 2o tbsp. dried mini fish heads, optional

Directions:

1. In a large microwaveable bowl, mix cereals, noodles, almonds, and fish heads.
2. In a small microwavable bowl, microwave butter and peanut butter uncovered on High about 20 seconds or until melted.

Stir in soy sauce, ginger, garlic powder, mustard, and sugar. Pour over cereal mixture until evenly coated.
3. Microwave uncovered on High for 4 minutes, thoroughly stirring every 2 minutes. Spread on waxed paper to cool, about 15 minutes.
4. Place in serving bowl and mix in popcorn.

If using an oven, follow above directions, but instead of microwaving, bake at 250 degrees for 25 minutes and stir every 15 minutes.

SNACK MIX EXTRAORDINAIRE

Ingredients:

¼ cup butter
4 tsp. Worcestershire sauce
1 tsp. salt
1 tsp. garlic powder
½ tsp. onion powder
1 tsp. papricka
¼ tsp. sugar
7 cups rice or corn cereal squares, or a combination of the two
1 cup peanuts
1 cup pretzels
1 cup oyster crackers

Directions:

1. In a large microwaveable bowl, mix cereals, peanuts, crackers, and pretzels then set aside.
2. In a separate microwaveable bowl, melt butter. Stir in

Worcestershire sauce, salt, garlic powder, onion powder, sugar, and paprika. Mix into bowl with dry ingredients and coat well.
3. Microwave uncovered on High for 6 minutes, thoroughly stirring every 2 minutes. Spread on waxed paper to cool, about 15 minutes.

If using an oven, follow above directions, but instead of microwaving, bake at 250 degrees for 1 hour and stir every 15 minutes.

MAXINE

CAPTAIN MUCCIN

A fairy tale ends with "they live happily ever after," and my sea story (this ain't no s**t) starts out in 1977 as a cadet aboard a modern American break bulk ship on the West Coast of South America in sunny Callao, Peru.

This was our second ship as cadets, so we now viewed ourselves as seasoned cadets and quasi mariners. In the 1970s, general cargo break bulk vessels would typically stay almost a week in a port loading and discharging cargo. Beautiful Callao, Peru, was no different.

As cadets, a week in a particular port gave us a lot of shore time. We definitely used it wisely. Our shipmates informed us that Callao had a wonderful marketplace, so one day we ventured to it. True to their word, it contained a conglomeration of all types of activities. Vendors were hawking everything imaginable, from local clothing, hats, knick-knacks, and electronics, to food and exotic animals and pets.

Somewhere through my meandering with the engine cadet, I ran across a merchant that was selling dogs. As a teenager with a fondness for dogs, I took a liking to a cute puppy. Before I knew it, the vendor had convinced me to purchase it, and I was on my way back to the ship with a small crate and the dog who I had named Maxine. She was as cute and cuddly as you could find.

Back in that era, or as we say those days, there was no gangway watch, etc… so we just climbed up the gangway and went to the cabin that we shared.

Then the engine cadet and myself set up a small box with linen for the dog and gave it water and food. Little did we know of the saga we would be in for.

We would tend to the dog when we could during the day and always made sure it had plenty of water, as it was hot in Peru.

Our first night with the dog was uneventful other than the dog would bark or howl every once in a while. We attributed it to her missing her mother and went out of our way to comfort her until she fell back to sleep.

Little did we know that the next morning while at breakfast in the officer's saloon (mess room) the chief mate mentioned he heard howling during the night. He then responded to himself that he must have been dreaming. We both agreed and went about eating our breakfast.

The same scenario continued for a few days, but every night it was getting better and was less frequent. We continued to make light of it with the chief mate and mentioned where we were docked they had wild dogs on the pier etc… that he might be hearing.

As our cabin was adjacent to the chief mate's cabin, we had to be extra careful of noise. We were getting a little paranoid but thought we had the issue handled.

A few days later while on our way to the next port, a crew member mentioned off the cuff that U.S. Customs was tough about bringing contraband such as pets into the U.S. We both starting thinking seriously that maybe we had made a mistake and that we would never be able to get the dog into the U.S.

So thinking quickly at this point, we decided that when we pulled into port the next day, we would see if we could find the puppy a good home. Unfortunately, we had no plan and it was a foreign port. Basically we were going to wing it and hope for the best.

What transpired next was really a miracle. The next morning after an early breakfast, we took off down the gangway and decided to visit every ship tied up on our pier. Little did we know that we would only have to go to one ship.

The first ship was a Russian break bulk vessel, and we boarded the gangway quickly with no one being present. As it was a Saturday, the longshoremen weren't working, so we decided to enter the amidships house and go to the galley where we hoped to find some crew members. Being lucky, we ran across a mate and asked to speak to the captain. He was close by and within a few moments we were having a friendly conversation, and he was fluent in English. We mentioned that we had purchased a small dog and needed to find it a new home. Before he could even answer, his family came into the galley including his wife and two small children. They did not speak English, but he translated to them our request, and I could tell by the smiles on the children and their excitement that we might have gotten lucky!

Within short order, the captain said his family wanted the puppy. So, quickly we indicated before he could change his mind that we would be back in a few minutes. We departed the ship and ran back to our ship, packed up the puppy and all the stuff we had for her, and headed back.

It was love at first sight, and the Captain's children were crazy for the dog. We had become attached to Maxine and were forlorn but happy she had found a good home. It all worked out in the end.

Later on during the voyage, we told our chief mate what we had done and thought we would get in big trouble, but he laughed and said we were young and had good hearts and did the right thing.

Smooth seas and following winds!

PART NINE
DRINKS

SETH LUCAS

I recall on one particular cruise my fellow cadet and friend, Steve Thompson, had left a large thermos of Kool Aid in the engine room of the TSES VI after watch. The next day we went on leave in London, so he did not retrieve his thermos until departure. While sitting in his stateroom that day, the lid sudden exploded off of the thing like a bomb. I'm not sure I want to know the source of the yeast (gross), but we had about a half gallon of fermented Kool Aid to kick-off the trip back home.

Subsequent to this batch, I have made several gallons of bilge wine to fill the down time at sea. A little bread yeast, some grape juice, and honey makes for a bold yet familiar blend that stings the palate and shocks the mind.

SUN TEA

Ingredients:

2 qts. of water in a sealable glass or plastic container
4-8 tea bags depending on desired strength. Flavor is a personal preference. Herbal or regular.
Slices of lemon or sprigs of mint (Optional)

Directions:

1. Pour water into your container, hang the teabags in ensuring that the labels are outside of the container. Seal the container and let sit in the sun for 4-6 hours. You may have to move location as the sun moves across the sky.
2. About an hour before taking in, place either lemon slices or mint sprigs (preferably in a tea infuser) into the tea.
3. When you bring in the tea, you can either leave the tea bags and your lemon or mint in the tea or remove them before placing in the fridge to cool.

VIKING EGGNOG

HANDS DOWN THE BEST EGGNOG YOU WILL EVER TASTE

Ingredients:

12 large eggs, separated
1½ cups superfine sugar
1 quart whole milk
1½ quarts heavy cream
3 cups bourbon
½ cup dark rum
2 cups cognac
Freshly grated nutmeg

Directions:

1. In a very large bowl, beat egg yolks until thick and pale yellow.
2. Gradually add sugar to yolks.
3. With a wire whisk, beat in milk and 1 quart cream.
4. Add bourbon, rum, and cognac, stirring constantly.
5. Just before serving, beat egg whites until stiff. Fold into mixture.

6. Whip remaining heavy cream until stiff and fold in. Sprinkle with nutmeg.

Hand your keys to a loved one and don't attempt to drive!

HOOCH

Ingredients:

1¾ liters scotch
1 cup oats
1 pound honey
2 cinnamon sticks
2 pints water
Should all fit in growler

Directions:

Just shake and mix multiple times a day for a week. Drain oats through a strainer after a week.

GREEN MONSTER

Ingredients:

2 lbs. spinach
2½ lbs. kale
2 lbs. celery
1 lb. cucumber
3 oz. ginger
2 gal. apple juice
1 gal. water

Directions:

Blanch greens to make them tender. Put everything in a blender and thoroughly blend.

Makes 5 gallons and last up to two 2 days refrigerated.

KAHLUA

Ingredients:

4 cups sugar
2 oz. instant coffee
1 pint hot water
1 pint cheap brandy
1 vanilla bean

Directions:

1. Mix 4 cups sugar and instant coffee in a pot.
2. Add the hot water and brandy. Heat thoroughly.
3. Pour mixture into a heated ½ gallon bottle.
4. Add the vanilla bean.
5. Shake every day for 30 days.

This fills 2 fifth bottles. It makes a great Christmas present tied up in red cellophane with a pretty bow.

MULLED CIDER

Ingredients:

¾ firmly packed brown sugar
1 tsp. cloves
1 tsp. allspice
1 tsp. cinnamon
¼ tsp. salt
One gallon cider

Directions:

1. Add spices to cider.
2. Heat thoroughly.
3. This drink is best served when steaming hot in earthen mugs.

MULLED WINE

Ingredients:

1 qt. red wine
1 lemon
10 whole cloves
1 stick cinnamon
Sugar to taste

Directions:

Cut gashes into the skin of the lemon and insert the whole cloves. Roast lemon for three minutes in hot oven. Heat wine with roasted lemon and cinnamon stick. Add sugar to tase and serve in a warm punch bowl. Cut lemon into slices for garnishing.

PREPARING FOR SEA

<u>The Load Line Promise</u>

"I understand the L.L.L. to be the symbol or sign for three things which I must never neglect, and these things are: Lead, Log and Look-out.

I believe in the Lead, as it warns me against dangers which the eye cannot see.

I believe in the Log, as it checks my distance run.

I believe in the Look-out, as it warns me against dangers to be seen.

The Lead warns me against dangers invisible, the Log warns me against false distances, and the Look-out warns me against dangers visible. And I earnestly resolve, and openly declare, that as I hope to sail my ship in safety on the ocean, as I wish to spare the lives of my fellow creatures at sea and as I wish to go in safety all my days, so will I steadfastly practice that which I believe."

Going to sea for either a few weeks or a few months requires planning and packing. A seasoned mariner will always repack after returning home after doing whatever laundry is necessary and have the bag ready to go at a moment's notice. The below is not exhaustive, but a great starting point.

Bringing your own entertainment is a good idea if it is a new vessel. Movies, books, computers, cards, etc. all help to pass the time. If you are bringing books and movies on a hard drive, back that information up on at least one other hard drive, preferably two, and leave one at home in case the worst case scenario hits and your bags get destroyed in transit.

- Multi tool (Leatherman, Gerber, etc.)
- Serrated knife
- Red lens flashlight
- White flashlight
- Baseball cap you don't mind losing
- UV A/B polarized sunglasses (2 pair)
- Prescription glasses with spares
- Your own coffee mug (plastic with a lid)
- 1 week worth of underwear and undershirts
- 2 weeks worth of socks
- Civilian clothing and at least one set of nice clothing; you never know when you need it. Khakis, shirt, and tie.
- Good insoles with spares to change out several times for your work boots
- Shower shoes
- Plenty of spare razor blades to match your razor
- Enough toiletries to last several months if you have sensitive skin. Most ships have soap, but you will need shampoo, toothpaste, etc.
- Several spare toothbrushes
- Sweater for watch
- Sweater you do not care wearing on deck and getting dirty
- Long johns or warm underwear
- Toiletry essentials (deodorant, baby powder, athlete's foot medicine, Benadryl, aspirin, antacid)
- Spare shoe and boot laces
- Batteries for flashlights

- Sewing kit
- First aid kit
- Gallon size ziploc bags (quality, not cheap ones)
- Paracord and duct tape for securing items in room
- Plenty of preferred feminine hygiene products
- If you take prescription medication, enough medication for the length of your contract with more to spare.

LIFE ON BOARD

Good relationships make the life of all seafarers more comfortable, healthy, and less prone to accidents. The elements which help in better relationships are:

- policies of company
- function of shipboard management
- clarity of responsibilities with reference to shipboard
- functions
- structure and flow of authority
- importance of understanding needs:
- individual needs
- ship needs
- company needs
- social needs

Everyone should respect each other's individuality, value, culture and purpose of work. Open communication will enhance IPR.

Even the most technically sophisticated shipboard environment demands better interpersonal relationships from seafarers during both on-duty or off-duty hours.

The methods to improve IPR on board are:

- introducing and understanding each other
- commitment of senior officers
- valuing of individual differences rather than maximizing weakness
- fairness in dealing with personnel
- true appraisals and reporting
- discipline on board

THE TEAM

A **team is** a group of people working together toward a common goal. Shipboard operation is teamwork and effectiveness, and it depends on the effectiveness of the team member. Team helps in better decision making.

TEAM BUILDING

The process for creating a new team is different from developing an existing team.

COLLABORATION

Collaboration is the lifeblood of any team. Collaboration is the act of **working effectively with others** to achieve a common goal. It needs to be built on trust, which can only be achieved through **honesty, openness, consistency, and respect.**

Honesty means that team members tell one another the truth, not just what each wants to hear. They feel comfortable disclosing problems so that other members can join in the problem-solving process and help overcome obstacles.

Openness means that team members are not afraid to say what is on their minds; they do not fear repercussions for communicating their thoughts. They share information because they are confident that people won't make fun of their ideas.

Consistency means that each team member works and interacts in a consistent manner. This allows members of the team to know what to expect from one another. Progress toward a goal can suffer when team members are inconsistent with their work, meeting attendance, communication, or even mood.

Respect means that team members see one another as vital parts of the team. They speak and behave respectfully toward one another. They listen to everyone's ideas without judgment, and offer constructive criticism.

BARRIERS TO TEAM EFFECTIVENESS

Effective teamwork can benefit the shipboard operations with improved communication, broader collaboration and a greater sense of accountability to the group. But there are barriers to effective teamwork that need to be identified and eliminated as follows:

- distortion of aims
- inflexible behavior of members
- groupism
- status/ego problems
- hidden agendas
- communication problems
- physical/environmental problems
- handling of grievances/counseling

BAD EXAMPLE OF TEAM EFFECTIVENESS:

Sailing as Chief mate on a research vessel, we had a 1st engineer who was territorial of his spot in the officers' mess. Most ships will say that there is no assigned seating, but get to know who prefers to sit where and try to avoid taking their spot. Doing so purposely can result in the following story.

The third mate knew where the 1st liked to sit during meals and sat there anyway, thinking the 1st had already eaten. As the mess was a small room, there were not many choices left as to where to sit. The 1st entered mid-meal and started screaming when he saw the third mate in "his spot." This resulted in a chair being thrown and a fight resulting. Both officers were censured by the captain, and this is a perfect interpersonal relationship of bad teamwork. The third could have sat elsewhere, but at fault was the 1st for expecting a specific seat to always be empty in case he walked in.

TEAM WORK

Teamwork is essential on board for reasons such as:

- The shipping company comprises a number of small mobile industrial units (the ship) which may at any particular moment be distributed over large distances throughout the world.
- When making a voyage, the ship can undergo considerable climatic changes, which may adversely affect personnel.
- Ships are operational for 24 hours each day, and the crew must be organized in regulated shift system, such that the people on board are well rested and fit for duty at all times.
- The personnel on the ship must be organized to operate the ship safely and effectively with numerous operations being performed simultaneously, e.g.

- watch keeping at sea and in port (navigation and machinery operation)
- cargo operations
- maintenance of hull, machinery and equipment
- safety checks and drills, emergency actions
- repair/dry-docking
- stocking provisions, cooking food, housekeeping
- communication ship - shore – ship
- the crew must be able to operate with a high degree of responsibility and flexibility

CULTURAL DIFFERENCES

Life at sea can be an adventure. Traveling to new places and meeting new people can be fun and challenging at the same time. We live in a culturally diverse world and country. The new mariner will quickly learn that even between New England and Texas there are a number of subtle and not so subtle differences, just as between Seattle and Dubai. It is important to be open to these experiences and respect the culture of those around us. Not understanding and respecting them can result in a misunderstanding with very drastic consequences.

COMMUNICATION ON BOARD

FUNDAMENTALS OF COMMUNICATION

Good communication is the most essential element of safety and pollution prevention on board. People's co-operation can be achieved by effective communication. Effective communication is the basic element for human survival. Language is a means of transmitting ideas, views, instructions, etc.

METHODS OF COMMUNICATION

The basic elements of communication are:

- Sender
- Receiver
- Modes of transmission
- Methods of transmission
- Barriers to communication
- Feedback

Feedback is essential in ship's communication. The following methods of communication may be classified under the following heads:

- Verbal, e.g. reading, speaking, writing and any communication using words
- Non-verbal, e.g. body language, sounds, gestures
- Iconic, e.g. signs, figures, diagrams, pictures and photographs

All three methods need to be effectively used on board for proper understanding. Verbal communication includes all communication pertaining to words, including reading, writing and speaking. Body language and pictorial symbols are more powerful means of communication than verbal means alone.

BARRIERS OF COMMUNICATION

There are barriers in each step of the basic communication process. These barriers are:

- Transmitter's conceptualization stage
- Transmitter's capability
- Mode of transmission
- Media of transmission
- Receiver's capability
- Receiver's understanding of the concept
- Feedback stage
- Receipt of feedback by transmitter

EFFECTIVE TRANSMISSION SKILLS

Effectiveness of communication lies primarily with the sender. The sender should define the purpose of the particular communication. It is important to use an appropriate vocabulary particularly in the English language (Maritime English).

Understanding the different kinds of barriers in communication helps in better transmission. The sender must be capable of effectively speaking, writing, acting, drawing and using available sound signaling apparatus. For effective communications, when the sender of a message communicates with the receiver, there has to be a correlation between what the sender is thinking about and what the receiver is thinking about.

Text or words must therefore be used in a consistent way, and the first requirement for communication is a set of messages that are used consistently. Effectiveness of transmission can be checked by the feedback from the receiver. This responsibility lies with the sender.

The typical length of a message, for both sender and receiver, is ultimately restricted by the amount of information that a person can handle at one time.

Much longer sentences can often only be understood only if they are easily decomposable to shorter sentences, so a vocabulary made up of shore terms or phrases that can be combined will probably have a greater chance of success.

EFFECTIVE LISTENING SKILLS

Listening is the responsibility of the receiver. However, listening and hearing are very different concepts.

Hearing is an involuntary process that starts with noise, vibrations, the movement of fluid in the ears and sound sent to the brain. Where it gets a little complicated is when the noise actually arrives at its final destination: the brain! This is where listening happens.

Listening is a voluntary act where we try to make sense out of the noise we hear. That could be your partner telling you to rake the leaves or your boss droning on about the latest plummeting sales figures. But the worst is when a speaker is on stage vying for your attention. In any event, hearing and listening are very different because listening requires conscious action.

Barriers are influencing factors which impede or break down the continuous communications loop.

They block, distort, or alter the information.

By identifying the barriers and applying countermeasures, team members can effectively communicate. Barriers include:

- Non-assertive behavior
- Task-preoccupation
- Anger or frustration
- Personal bias
- Team diversity
- Lack of confidence
- Inappropriate priorities
- Organizational structure
- Distractions
- Tunnel vision
- Interruptions
- Rank differences

Human beings are capable of speaking at a rate of 150 words per minute, whereas they can listen at a rate of about 1 000 wpm.

This results in idle time of 850 wpm, which makes the mind wander. Ideally this idle time should be used for paraphrasing the body language and other signals from the speaker

EFFECTS AND CONSEQUENCES OF WRONG COMMUNICATION

Wrong communication can affect safety of life, property and the environment, human problems and problems in relationships on board. Improper communication causes stress, loss of time, loss of resources and even ship's profitability.

COMMUNICATION SUM-UP

Effective communication creates the atmosphere conducive to safe working, happy living, and sociable relationships among fellow shipmates. Habits, values, and attitudes can also be modified by effective communication and knowing the basics of interpersonal relationships, learning skills and team skills.

ACKNOWLEDGEMENTS

Special thanks to my test cook and photographers:
Kathryn Brewer and Kristal Soo

Story Masters:
Keith Gibney, Emil Muccin, Erik Larsen, Thomas Powers, P. Michael DeCharles, Roy Love, Crystal Allen

Test Cooks:
Kathryn Brewer, Kristal Soo, Sophie Tirrel, Nicholas Barnes, Amanda Yeam, Anita Bonvento

Thanks for your contributions go to:
Lilianna Di Gesu
Christopher Soo
Michael Chalos
Steven Chernow
Brian Abbott
Christopher Shaw
Russel Avolio
Elaina Davis
John Tylawsky
Danielle Centeno
Daniel Kiernan
George Sherier
Paul Cummings
Amie Carter
AJ Adams
Justin Gaithard
Brian Hennesy
Ed Ryzner
Evan Goldshlag
Joseph Mastrogiovani
Carolyn Hunter
Sarah Bulucluc
Pat Bless
Alexandra Hagerty
Lisa Chiu
Roger Bing
Lindsay Price
Carl Hausheer
Dotty Chesebrough
Eileen Famine
Frank Kollman
Eric Johannson
Edward Licio Poian
Erik Larsen
Andrew Higgins
Brian Fleming

S. M. Patricola
Bradley Golden
Christine Klimkowsi
Roderick Acquie
John Knauss
Joe Heller
Scott Philips
Jordan Bistany
Stephanie Reuger
Peggy Fitch
Richard Ohlsen
Jeffrey Perlstein
Ashanti Storr
Mark Pellegrino
Jimmy Zatwarnicki
Zhen Lin
Jim Rogin
Barbara Jean Reggio
Keith Gibney
Carol Cerny
Brian Brown
Justin Rosenschein
Debbie Lindman
Vanessa Robert
Vivian Cruise
Dawn Contreras
Abigail Thomas

LET THERE BE NO MOANING AT THE BAR

Old sailors sit
And chew the fat
About things that used to be,
Of the things they've seen,
The places they've been,
When they ventured out to sea.

They remembered friends
From long ago,
The times they had back then,
The money they spent,
The beer they drank,
In their days as sailing men.

Their lives are lived
In the days gone by
With the thoughts that forever last.
Of the bell bottom blues,
Round white hats,
And good times in their past.

*They recall long nights
With the moon so bright
Far out into the lonely sea.
The thoughts they had
As youthful lads,
When their lives were wild and free.*

*They know so well
How their hearts would swell
When the flag fluttered proud and free.
The underway pennant
Such a beautiful sight
As they plowed through an angry sea.*

*They talked of the scran
the chefs would make
And the shrill of the bosuns pipe.
How salt spray would fall
Like sparks from hell
When a storm struck in the night.*

*They remember old shipmates
Already gone
Who forever hold a spot in their heart,
When sailors were bold,
And friendships would hold,
Until death ripped them apart.*

*They speak of nights
Spent in bawdy houses
On many foreign shore,
Of the beer they'd down
As gathering around,
Telling jokes with a busty whore.*

*Their sailing days
Are gone away,*

Never again will they cross the brow.
They have no regrets,
They know they are blessed,
For honoring the sacred vow.

Their numbers grow less
With each passing day
As the final muster begins,
There's nothing to lose,
All have paid their dues,
And they'll sail with shipmates again.

I've heard them say
Before getting underway
That there's still some sailing to do,
They'll say with a grin that their ship has come in,
And the Good Lord is commanding the crew.

www.ingramcontent.com/pod-product-compliance
Lightning Source LLC
Chambersburg PA
CBHW072149070526
44585CB00015B/1056